Alternative Programs for Disruptive Youth

Edited by

M. Angele Thomas,
The Council for
Exceptional Children

David A. Sabatino,
Southern Illinois University
at Carbondale

Rosemary C. Sarri,
University of Michigan

A Product of the ERIC Clearinghouse
on Handicapped and Gifted Children

The Council for Exceptional Children

A product of the ERIC Clearinghouse on Handicapped and Gifted Children.

Published in 1982 by The Council for Exceptional Children, 1920 Association Drive, Reston, Virginia 22091.

Library of Congress Number 81–71935

ISBN 0–86586–124–2

The material in this publication was prepared pursuant to contract no. 400–76–0119 with the National Institute of Education, U.S. Department of Education. Contractors undertaking such projects under Government sponsorship are encouraged to express freely their judgment in professional and technical matters. Prior to publication, the manuscript was critically reviewed for determination of professional quality. Points of view or opinions, however, do not necessarily represent the official view or opinions of either the clearinghouse's parent organization or the National Institute of Education.

Printed in the United States of America.

Contents

Preface

The most obvious reason why students drop out is to get away from school. Whatever causes them to feel threatened, insecure, uncomfortable, unsuccessful, alienated, or belligerent must be changed. If we want to do something constructive for young people who are prone to drop out, we must be willing to modify our traditional concepts of secondary schools. Alternative programs are one possible answer. The purpose of this book is to provide information about a variety of alternative education programs that are working effectively with disruptive youth.

This population has been a targeted concern of The Council for Exceptional Children for many years. One of its Divisions, the Council for Children with Behavioral Disorders, has 5,000 members. Publications have been produced on managing inappropriate behavior. Conferences have been conducted on children with serious emotional disturbance; learning and behavior problems of handicapped students in secondary schools; and education's responsibility for disruptive, alienated, and incarcerated youth. All of these activities and the cadre of people involved helped identify alternative programs around the country. CEC staff contacted the program directors and requested a response to certain questions about their schools. The editors then screened the information for appropriate inclusion in the publication.

The book is in response to the needs of the schools to develop adequate programs. Its intended audience includes program developers, directors, supervisors, principals, and other building and district administrators who are responsible for setting the tone and direction of innovations and improvements in school programs. The nation's critical problems with chronically disruptive youth and the schools' lack of initiative in assuming responsible leadership in effective programming are prevalent. Unacceptable behavior frequently results in the administration's taking action to suspend or expel pupils from the regular instructional program. On the other hand, an element common to successful alternative programs is the strong support of administrators.

The book has five sections. In the Introduction, Rosemary C. Sarri, Professor of Social Work, University of Michigan, draws upon her experience with the problems of chronically disruptive youths and the people who impact upon their lives. She explains that the effectiveness of alternative education programs in reducing malperformance and delinquency depends on how well the alternatives are conceived and implemented. If they are conceived of only as a social control mechanism for those students already in difficulty, they are not likely to be effective for prevention purposes, nor will they lead to needed modifications in traditional school programs.

The second section is authored by David A. Sabatino, Professor and Chairperson, Department of Special Education, Southern Illinois University at Carbondale, who has written extensively on norm-violating youth of high school age. He addresses some critical issues and concerns such as the general lack of formal efficacy studies that would definitively establish one approach over all others. Despite this need, certain programs succeed at least part of the time with some of their students, and their functional value is convincing.

The third section of the book compiles detailed information about four alternative programs. None is singled out as THE model. None promises a miraculous cure. They all provide descriptions characterizing target population, class placement, program resources, program content, student management, program evaluation, and program funding. The examples cited are representative of numerous others, and many of the programs share common components.

The fourth section follows the same outline of organization as the third section. However, only brief overviews are provided for 12 alternative programs, since space did not allow us to print extended descriptions of all 16 programs.

Finally, the Appendix contains citations of reference materials, teacher manuals, referral procedures, accreditation reports, handbooks of information, and operational guidelines that the various programs use. These materials may be ordered from the ERIC Document Reproduction Service, Box 190, Arlington, Virginia 22010. Consult *Resources in Education* for the ED ordering number and cost of each document. Directors' and/or principals' names, addresses, and phone numbers are also provided in the text for anyone wishing to make direct contact with a particular program. All of the individuals contributing to this volume are to be commended for their commitment to students who have difficulty with traditional school programs. If their attempts at alternative interventions have reduced the number of juvenile offenders going into courts or correctional institutions, there is hope that others will do likewise.

M. Angele Thomas

CHAPTER 1

Introduction

ROSEMARY C. SARRI

Recent reports at both state and national levels have aroused considerable concern about the educational performance of American youth. Despite the investment of substantial resources, findings from the evaluation of educational programs as well as the performance of youth are disappointing. They clearly indicate that some fundamental thinking about contemporary approaches to elementary and secondary education is urgently needed. Nonetheless any new innovations will have to be implemented with reduced resources since it is also clear that the allocation of resources will remain stable at best, but is more likely to continue on its present downward spiral.

Increasing numbers of youth are at serious risk today because of poverty, family disorganization, educational handicaps, substance abuse, mental illness, delinquency, premature parenting and, last but certainly not least, serious and persistent unemployment for youth and young adults. These problems provoked Kadish (1968) to contend that children and youth were the newest minority group in the United States.

Adolescence is a time for experimentation with new lifestyles, philosophies, and modes of behavior. Our society does not provide legitimate opportunities for these youth. Instead of encouraging and tolerating their experimentation, which may produce far more productive and capable adults, we subject them to rigid authority. We require in our crowded urban communities high levels of conformity to adult behavior and lifestyles, thus creating an almost perfect set-up for frustration and hostility. It is not surprising that young adults respond to this situation with even more hostility and/or alienation. In turn,

1

society attempts greater control—a self-defeating strategy at best. It is essential, therefore, that we examine some of the key social institutions in this society to ascertain how their current functioning might be changed to increase their effectiveness in the socialization of youth. Obviously, the school is one of these institutions.

THE SCHOOL IN CONTEMPORARY SOCIETY

The public school was once the key institution in the assimilation of rural and immigrant youth into an industrializing society. With the growth of the service-oriented society, the functions of the school changed, but more recently the change in the energy situation and the loss of world leadership in industrial output suggests to many that the United States must educate its youth more effectively for the future if leadership is to be restored. From one point of view, the schools are still agents for the maintenance of the societal status quo. In fact, Parsons (1966) viewed "pattern maintenance" as the primary function of the school.

In Western society a number of longstanding myths about education have recently been dispelled. For a long time the myth was that the key to success, upward mobility, and the good life was through education. Most believed that education could prepare people for opportunities and that persons were not integrated into the mainstream because they were not prepared—not educated. It was thought that all that was necessary was to provide equality of educational opportunity. However, research and the experience of minority groups and women showed clearly that equality of educational opportunity was often not available. Jencks (1972) and others have noted that education often is not positively correlated with income and other measures of successful achievement.

A longitudinal study by Levin (1976) in several Western European countries was even more persuasive. Education was examined in terms of equality of access, equality of educational participation, equality of educational results, and equality of educational effects on life chances. He concluded that if equality of educational opportunity is viewed as a mechanism for social mobility or to assure that all talents will be found, developed, and allocated on the basis of merit, then the results are nearly the opposite of those anticipated.

These critiques are serious because they challenge long-held ideologies. Havighurst (1976) suggested that rather than focusing on equality of educational opportunity, we should focus on equality of educational outcomes. He stated that all youth (excluding those who are seriously handicapped) can master the secondary school curriculum and, therefore, a strategy of equal end products makes sense. Moreover, secondary school should prepare persons for a meaningful life,

2

not just for further education or an occupation. Public schools, said Havighurst, have more promise for poor children and poor children have more need of public schools than anyone else. Yet, Ernest Boyer, former U.S. Commissioner of Education, reported that in 1979 25% of all high school students left school before they were graduated (Washington Crime News Service, June 1, 1979:2). The Children's Defense Fund (1980) reported that thousands of elementary school children never enter secondary schools. These youth are disproportionately from poor, disadvantaged, minority, and single-parent families who lack resources to see that their children are fully educated.

A related problem confronting schools today is the emphasis on credentialism. School credentials are increasingly becoming the single most important requirement for upward mobility. The situation becomes particularly problematic for youth who do not complete secondary school, and in many communities of the United States today, fewer than 50% who enter high school graduate 4 years later. One must inevitably ask: For what kind of life are school dropouts being prepared? Departments and Boards of Education have an obligation to provide a positive answer to that question. The situation becomes a Catch 22 in that the employment system increasingly excludes youth without a high school diploma or its equivalent. Such youth thus experience discrimination on the basis of schooling rather than being evaluated on the basis of whether or not they are capable of performing the particular job at issue. Characterized by a worship of credentials, the system blocks all entry into the work situation or up the ladder. One youth described it aptly: "After they gave me all the tests and said that I could fill out the employment papers, they came back in a few minutes and said that I couldn't because I didn't have a diploma" (Sarri & Vinter, 1974).

Recent actions by unions to close membership and discourage apprenticeships gives further indication of the seriousness of the situation. The public schools and agencies charged with youth welfare can best attack this problem effectively. Cooperative efforts by local, state, and federal governments as well as by voluntary and private educational organizations are also necessary.

One of the most exciting and effective mechanisms for aiding youth who have had difficulty with traditional secondary education in the United States has been the alternative school. This mechanism has been in existence for a long period of time in a variety of forms—primarily for vocational education, but also for special education for disadvantaged, handicapped, delinquent, or malperforming youth. Since the mid-sixties, the term *alternative education* has been used widely to refer to more flexible educational structures that focus greater attention on individualized and experimental education for the students it serves. However, as long ago as 1902 John Dewey experimented with innovative alternative structures, and in the 1950's Neill's

3

Summerhill School attracted much attention. Later, in the 1960's, a number of street academies, free schools, and tutorial programs developed in several states. Some of these schools were designed for inner-city youth who had been expelled or dropped out or were achieving below expectations, while others were for middle class, suburban youth who were disillusioned with traditional approaches. Gradually public schools saw these innovations as desirable and developed their own alternatives. By 1978 the National Alternative Schools program identified 1,300 alternative school programs in the 50 states (Flaxman & Homstead, 1978).

WHAT IS AN ALTERNATIVE SCHOOL?

Alternative education is variously conceived and defined. It might be as brief as an experience in a tutorial or remedial program for a few weeks or as long as a comprehensive learning program of several years, as several of the communities in this publication report. Several elements appear to be found in most thorough-going alternative education programs. First, they are designed for individualized instruction, tailored to a student's needs and interests, with clearly stated goals and a plan for their achievement to which the student agrees. Second, there must be a clear system of rewards for both effort and output. Programs are usually small in size with low student-teacher ratios. Teachers are expected to develop positive and caring relationships with students. Finally, the school's administration must establish a climate of respect, with fair and just disciplinary procedures. Some alternative schools may also have parental as well as student involvement in curriculum. Social work services are often provided to help students handle personal and social problems. Experiential learning and transition experiences to young adult roles in the community are considered essential components in many alternative schools. Most alternative programs place high value on innovation, creativity, flexibility, and participatory decision-making between students and staff. In nearly all instances, alternative education is conceived of as a means for promoting education and social development for youths who have encountered difficulties in traditional educational structures (Gold, 1978).

The effectiveness of alternative education programs in reducing school malperformance, delinquency, and other disruptive behavior depends at least in part on how well the alternatives are conceived and implemented. Many programs have been developed only to handle specific problems created for the school because of the disruptive behavior of certain youth. If programs are conceived of only as a social control mechanism for those already in difficulty, they are not likely to be effective for prevention purposes, nor will they lead to needed modifications in traditional school programs. Rather, alternative schools will be identified only as places for "hard-core," "problem," or "disruptive" youth. Individual rather than organizational characteristics will be viewed as the critical causative factors. The findings from Fizzell's (1979) study of alternative schools in Chicago indicated that individual student behavior improved, but there was almost no change in district-wide ratios of suspensions, truancies, or disruptive behavior. Fizzell argued that the program had almost no effect on overall school programs.

There is evidence, however, that alternative schools can reverse the process of educational malperformance and delinquency (Barr, Colston & Parrett, 1977; Gold, 1978; Polk & Schafer, 1972). Programs described in this book also indicate that there can be substantial improvement in academic achievement and satisfaction with school as well as increased attachment to school, while at the same time delinquency, dropping out, vandalism, and other disruptive behavior are reduced. All concur that a critical goal for alternative education is to increase opportunity for academic success without compromising educational standards. It can break the cycle of school failures, parental rejection, and delinquency (Elliott & Voss, 1974). Synthesis of the findings from numerous evaluations of alternative school programs in all parts of the United States suggests that the following elements are critical to success. Most of the programs described in this volume address these same elements in the design and implementation of their programs:

1. Goal-oriented learning and work in the classroom.
2. Individualized instruction with curricula that are tailored to individual interests and needs.
3. Clear rewards for individual improvement in academic competency.
4. Caring and competent teachers who develop warm and meaningful interpersonal relationships with students.
5. Strong and supportive leadership by the school administration that establishes the climate for implementation and is correlated with normative behavior by youth.
6. A small student population of 100 or fewer.
7. Low student-adult ratios, asserted by many to be the most critical element in achieving goal-oriented individualized instruction.
8. Flexibility, innovation, and a positive attitude toward change by the administration and staff that facilitates program effectiveness and increases student satisfaction.

All of these factors suggest that if alternative education is to succeed, school boards and administration must commit themselves to alternative educational modalities for a significant proportion of students and, perhaps, to some extent for all students. Many large public secondary schools in the United States have become highly bureaucratized, thereby hampering and sometimes preventing the achievement of the goals for which they were established. It is quite possible that in the future many elements from alternative education programs can be implemented into the mainstream of elementary and secondary schools, thereby improving education for all students.

REFERENCES

Barr, R., Colston, B., & Parrett, W. An analysis of six school evaluators: The effectiveness of alternative public schools. *Viewpoints*, 1977, *53*, 1–30.

Children's Defense Fund. *Massachusetts study finds juvenile detention a shocking throwback.* Washington, D.C., CDF Reports 1980, *2*, 7.4.

Elliott, D., & Voss, H. *Delinquency and dropout.* Lexington MA: D. C. Heath, 1974.

Fizzell, R. *The truants alternative program: An evaluation to the State Board of Education.* Macomb IL: Western Illinois University, 1979.

Flaxman, A., & Homstead, K. *National directory of public alternative schools.* Amherst MA: University of Massachusetts School of Education, 1978.

Gold, M. Scholastic experience, self-esteem, and delinquent behavior: A theory for alternative schools. *Crime and Delinquency*, 1978, *24* (3), 290–308.

Havighurst, R. Education policy for the large cities. *Social Problems*, 1976, *24*, 270–281.

Jencks, C. *Inequality: A reassessment of the effect of family and schooling in America.* New York: Basic Books, 1972.

Kadish, S. The dangers of overcriminalization. *The Annals of the New York Academy of Sciences*, 1968, 374:158–170.

Levin, H. Educational opportunities and social incarceration in Western Europe. *Social Problems*, 1976, *24*, 148–167.

Parsons, T. *Societies: Evolutionary and comparative perspectives.* Englewood Cliffs NJ: Prentice-Hall, 1966.

Polk, K., & Schafer, W. *Schools and delinquency.* Englewood Cliffs NJ: Prentice-Hall, 1972.

Sarri, R., & Vinter, R. Beyond group work: Organizational determinants of malperformance in secondary schools. In P. Glasser, R. Sarri, & R. Vinter (Eds.), *Individual change through small groups.* New York: Free Press, 1974, 431–458.

CHAPTER 2

Issues and Concerns:
Problems with Alternative Schools

DAVID A. SABATINO

In 1972 the National Schools Public Relations Association prepared a report entitled *Alternative Schools: Pioneering Districts Create Options for Students.* That report was an initial document on the state of the art of alternative programs for secondary students. It represented the first complete, single source reference to the nearly 200 alternative educational projects that were operating in the United States at that time.

The philosophy that gave the impetus to alternative programs literally came out of the woodwork. It was a bold new stance, reflecting the mood of the nation in the mid to late 1960's. This was the age of Aquarius, the overt search for personal freedom from the system. People were enjoying the fruits, if not the protection, of the system. However, many educators were opposed to so-called nontraditional educational alternatives for the following reasons:

1. They felt the traditional format with regular tracks (business, academic, etc.), special education, and vocational education provided reasonable alternatives reflecting the needs of society and, therefore, the future needs of the student.
2. They felt that opening the traditional system to self-indulged, voluntary, elected alternatives created a flexibility that endangered the student's future and that of society.

Underlying their feelings was the impact of the war in Vietnam, its social consequences, and the response of some of the nation's youth who protested by crossing the Canadian line in order to avoid their military obligation.

In short, *traditional school programs were viewed as successful because they reflected the times and were justified because they prepared students for entrance into the social order.* On the other hand, many secondary educators reasoned that an alternative educational program:

1. Allowed more alternatives than the students' decision-making capability, maturity, or experience permitted.
2. Led to a dead end by rejecting the importance of the 17 Carnegie Units needed for graduation and a successful life.
3. Questioned the authority of secondary educators, in that an expelled student would, in fact, have an alternative to the school's rules.
4. Reinforced students to refute the rules of society, to make their own rules, and to live in a house of glass, supported by the social order, while their very presence there amounted to throwing stones at those who pay the bills for this society.

In short, *the rationale for alternative programs was questioned by traditional secondary educators as a socialistic, valueless deterrent to a 200-year-old successful practice.*

The issue then, became what real educational value alternative programs offered to the student, society, and the educational community. Had an educational movement been instituted that was not based on data? On the contrary, alternative programs were developed because:

1. Traditional programs were *not* serving all youth satisfactorily (Coleman, 1966).
2. Of the secondary school-age youth 17.1% were dropped or stopped from attendance (Washington, 1973).
3. Of the secondary school-age youth 10.9% were reported to be handicapped, while 6.9% were in fact, being served (National Center for Educational Statistics, 1978).
4. The attitude of the traditional educator was one of focusing on the academic and vocational program, not on student function. Academic and vocational achievement was viewed as a privilege, not a right. Therefore, failure was seen by many to be a self-determined act of the student, not a factor beyond the control of the student.
5. Traditional programs treated all students equally, generally lock-stepping them into the same curricula regardless of ability, reading level, motivational factors, or social-personal adjustment factors (those variables identified with mild handicapping conditions).
6. Traditional programs emphasized the development of giftedness or talent and received financial support in keeping with society's priorities, that is, first for the gifted athlete; second, the academically talented; and third, the social rule-learner (i.e., the good kid).

7. Alternative programs could provide for ethnic, cultural, and linguistic differences; their development reflected a conviction that no one curriculum is suitable for *all* students *all* the time. "To insist that there is only one curriculum is to confuse the means of education with the end" (Silberman, 1970). The dropout rate for inner-city Blacks remains in excess of 30%, and for Spanish-speaking youth it reaches nearly 50% (Havighurst, 1970).
8. Alternative programs could provide students a choice, and frequently they could give the right to make and enforce rules to the majority (students), not the minority (school officials). Alternatives are a part of the American heritage, the opportunity to refute tradition and search for more self-fulfilling options.
9. Alternative programs frequently have not been full-blown alternatives to traditional programs. They have merely offered an "improvisational and in many instances, last-resort alternative program to those students who have failed to respond to conventional schooling" (Shanker, 1972, p. 4).
10. Alternatives are just that, various types of programs, not a specific program. Therefore, to talk in general about alternative curricula is really to discuss alternative*s* of program*s*—schools without walls, mini-schools, schools within schools, dropout centers, schools for special learners, open schools, ethnic-centered schools, or self-programming opportunities. The term *alternative school* is generic in the fullest sense of the word.

HOW EFFECTIVE ARE ALTERNATIVE SCHOOLS?

The purpose of the introduction was to establish the absence of specificity and the range of variation in goals and objectives of alternative programs. Those characteristics in themselves contribute to the difficulty of assessing the impact of alternative programs. Then too, alternative programs are generated by social conditions, the economic climate, the mood of the nation as reflected in its legislation and funding pattern, and finally by the educational communities' acceptance of change.

These variables are difficult to measure, but readily contribute to how effective an alternative program is perceived to be. Certainly, alternative programs are a type of educational experience, and in that sense they share the absence of definitive measurement of their effectiveness.

Generally, the critics of alternative programs contend that such programs must:

1. Provide basic skills.

9

2. Abide by the rules of a democratic society.
3. Employ a staff willing to work in a nontraditional atmosphere.
4. Avoid dependence on a few advocates.
5. Recognize the success and failures experienced by other alternative programs.
6. Provide certified programs leading to vocation or college entry.
7. Use innovative teaching approaches, not old procedures in new settings.
8. Inform the public and educational community of the program and its effects.
9. Avoid pampering students.
10. Avoid presenting a one-sided (the student's) point of view as an overreaction to traditional programs.
11. Collect data on effectiveness and efficiency.

How effective are alternative programs? The answer depends in part on what is being evaluated. Bremer and von Moschzisker (1971), writing on the evaluation of alternative programs, noted that a formative, day-to-day evaluation is necessary. Evaluation should provide corrective feedback on the practices of teachers and administrators. In that respect, evaluation has had almost no effect on the development of or improvement in educational programs. Bremer and von Moschzisker summarized their feelings, "Anything worth evaluating cannot be evaluated and anything that can be evaluated is not worth evaluating" (p. 122).

Bremer and von Moschzisker's point may be well taken, or as Cohen (1976) has stated, the service motive in special education has consistently outrun the scientific motive. Evaluation methodology should be structured into the school program at the onset. To evaluate is to measure. Any measurement lacks meaning unless the standard is known. Before students and schools can be properly evaluated, criteria must be established. To return to Cohen's premise, most alternative programs are initiated in response to a crisis awakening, usually to an old problem, for all the wrong reasons, that is, political or social, not educational. Therefore, educational criteria go unstated.

Evaluation requires definitive statements of purpose, with objectives couched in measurable criteria. For example, Seattle's Meary Middle School has five definite objectives with clearly stated and quantifiable criteria:

1. To reduce absenteeism by 20% from the previous year.
2. To reduce suspension by 20% from the previous year.
3. To raise reading by one grade level over the previous year.
4. To raise mathematics performance by one grade level over the previous year.
5. To improve students' self-concepts.

When such clear objectives and criteria are nonexistent, evaluation problems emerge.

Vincenzi and Fishman (1978) reviewed 75 alternative programs in Philadelphia and classified them into four types: disruptive/truant programs, career programs, individual programs, and nontraditional school pattern programs. There is not much clarity in the distinction or among the four classification structures. However, in that massive data collection process, examining attendance, behavior, and academic achievement over a 2-year period has demonstrated that students with previously poor attendance records were in school and progressing academically at a mean rate with those in traditional high schools.

Evaluation design differs from research design in that control groups are rarely used. Social and academic progress is based on general populations from regular high schools rather than on learners with similar characteristics in alternative programs. In an evaluation-research design on the Middle Years Alternative Program (MYA) in Ann Arbor, Michigan, two hypotheses were tested:

> First, that only minimal differences in achievement exist between students in alternative and traditional classrooms and second, that classroom setting does make a difference in preferred learning style. The evaluation was designed to measure five variables: (1) academic achievement; (2) student attitudes; (3) parent attitudes; (4) teacher/counselor attitudes; and (5) cognitive style. Measures of academic achievement were school attendance records and scores on the Michigan Educational Assessment Program (MEAP) and the California Achievement Test (CAT). ... There were no statistical differences on the academic and cognitive style measures between the 81 MYA students and two control groups: non-MYA students at the same school and a district-wide sample. Opinion survey responses indicated that all groups were generally enthusiastic about the program, but it was concluded that the MYA students did not necessarily have higher self concepts. (Thompson & Shein, 1978, p. 3)

Generally, then, alternative programs can claim academic achievement similar to that of traditional programs. Truancy is curbed dramatically; the dropout rate is generally reduced by up to one-third.

How successful are the students in returning to home schools? The return rate to regular programs is approximately one-fourth of the alternative population, with another one-fourth to one-half completing the alternative program (Simon, Levin, Fieldstone, & Johnson, 1973).

WHAT SHOULD BE EVALUATED?

Alternative schools, not unlike most educational programs, face an educational evaluation dilemma. The points of that dilemma are: (a) the program goals are different than the student goals; (b) the philosophy is rarely examined empirically, and it becomes an unchallenged acceptable; and (c) the student objectives are not analyzed statistically, but are reported on an individual and group frequency basis. Therefore, the data generally are *not* usable.

Consider a case in point, which is much more the rule than the exception when examining evaluation data. The evaluation was a 5-year-long review of an alternative education project with 2,000 to 2,500 students. The project goals were:

1. To base educational objectives on the needs and interests of the students.
2. To make sure that tasks assigned to reach these objectives are ones at which the students themselves can reasonably be expected (and expect) to succeed.
3. To structure the school program in such a way that if goals 1 and 2 are accomplished the objectives will be reached.

The project philosophy can be summarized as follows:

1. The student-teacher ratio has a significant effect on classroom learning.
2. The "I teach, you learn" relationship is not sacred.
3. The school and community offer a multitude of resources that are too frequently left untapped by the classroom teacher.
4. People learn to succeed by succeeding, and school activities should logically progress from one success to another.
5. The development of a positive self-concept is more important to the alienated school child than is any predetermined structured body of knowledge.
6. The positive aspects of school rewards and the negative aspects of school punishments have not been powerful enough motivating agents for a substantial number of students.
7. The student can profit from school experiences without being confined to an externally imposed, rigid curriculum.
8. Adequate time is required for teacher planning, observation, and evaluation of student performance.
9. To be effective, the teacher must allow himself or herself to be seen as a real person and must be willing to accept the risks and pains involved in this humanizing process.
10. More effective learning occurs when the student is involved in the initial choice of classroom activity than when the teacher controls all classroom options.
11. The cost of student-centered curricula is cheap in contrast to what the community and nation pay for unemployable and/or delinquent youth.
12. To be a significant person to students, the teacher must seek feedback from them and act accordingly.

13. A person's ego development is enhanced by having the opportunity to be heard and by seeing others respond positively to what is said.
14. Emotional stress frequently interferes with daily academic pursuits and must be dealt with before learning can occur.

The five measurable product objectives were:

1. By the end of the 1973–1974 school year, 60% of the students who had poor attendance records (absent more than 12.5% of days enrolled) during the previous school year will demonstrate at least a 10% comparative increase in the number of days attended or will reduce absence to fewer than 12.5% of days enrolled.
2. By the time of the final 1973–1974 posttest, 70% of the students who had ratings of 1, 2, or 3 on the *Self-Regarding Attitudes* scale pretest will demonstrate a positive change of at least one scale point in each of the specific self-regarding attitudes contained in the rating instrument.
3. By the time of the final 1973–1974 posttest, 70% of the student population will demonstrate *acceptable* performance (minimum rating of 3) and 30% of the student population will demonstrate *superior* performance (rating of 4 or 5) on at least four of the five behaviors specified on the *Self-Regarding Attitudes* rating instruments.
4. At the time of the final 1973–1974 posttest, at least 60% of the alternative student population who had pretest scores greater than one standard deviation below the norm on any subtest (reading, composition, math) will demonstrate improvement of at least five standard score points.
5. At the time of the final 1973–1974 posttest, at least 60% of the student population who had pretest scores between one-half and one standard deviation below the norm on any subtest (reading, composition, math) of the TAP will demonstrate improvement of at least two and one-half standard score points.

A summary of the project's progress (Blanchard, Knouff, & Nelsen, 1974), it seems, pays little attention to any of the student goals and presents a rather subjective opinion. We quote:

> Current progress of Management Component Objectives is *excellent*. Specifically, of the five management objectives, progress toward the accomplishment of four objectives (the enrollment of students, revision of the program operations manual, preparation of performance objectives, and preparation of a media production) has been excellent, and one objective (revision of the ... Curriculum Summary) good....
> Progress of Education/Training Objectives has been somewhat *mixed*. That is, of seven objectives, progress has been excellent on one (success experiences in instructional classes); good on another (acceptable and superior behavior performance); fair on a third (improvement in "posi-

13

tive self-regarding" behaviors); and undetermined on the remaining four (attendance improvement by poor attenders, average attendance of all ... students, basic skill improvement: students one standard deviation below norm, and basic skill improvement: students one-half standard deviation below norm). With respect to the acceptable and superior behavior performance objective, the alternative education staff has been able to increase the number of students demonstrating acceptable performance on each of the behaviors but has only been able to increase the number of students demonstrating superior performance in one of the behaviors. Progress has only been fair on the objective pertaining to improvement in "positive self-regarding" behaviors because the majority of students with initial ratings of three or less are still in need of improvement....

In conclusion, the overall progress of the ... project toward accomplishing its stated objectives has been *quite good.*

The data summary on student performance is unusable. For example, the table reporting student turnover fails to relate to any of the program objectives or student objectives (Table 1).

The summary statement on project effectiveness concludes the evaluation report. It takes a vindictive swipe at measurable objectives.

TABLE 1
Analysis of Student Turnover
Sept. '71–April '74

Disposition of case	Number of students
Returned to regular ... high school classes	51
Transferred to other [area] high schools	5
Family moved from [locale]	15
Transferred to other local institutions ... (community college, evening high school)	14
Married, left school	2
Left school for full-time employment	12
Dropped all educational programs and not working	7
Court assignment to group home	1
Assigned to home teacher due to extended illness	2
School Board expulsion	1
Currently enrolled	100
Total	210

From Blanchard, R. Knouff, W., & Nelsen, R., *Manual for developing a school-within-a-school alternative program.* Portland OR: Portland Public Schools, 1974.

Effectiveness

When speaking to the question of ... effectiveness, it must be pointed out that the terminal goals of the project are really no different than those of almost any other American secondary school. There is *nothing* innovative or exemplary about [the program] in terms of *product* objectives: the staff hopes to help youngsters to become proficient in the basic skills, to be capable of making sound decisions, to utilize effectively their leisure time, and to become, in general, happy, productive members of the society.

What *is* innovative and exemplary about [the project] are the *processes* by which the project approaches these common educational goals. It is in the areas of philosophy, organization, personal relationships, and operation that [the administration] hopes to demonstrate procedures and protocols which will serve as models for the national educational community.

It is unfortunate, therefore, that the national validation program is so exclusively concerned with measurable product objectives.

We wish that the evaluation report on this one project could be cited as a rare example. On the contrary, it tends to reflect a typical attitude of rebellious educators too busy criticizing the system, its standards, and its procedures (including evaluation devices), to offer an objective review of the project's work or worth.

ANTI-EVALUATION ATTITUDE

Bass (1978) provided a study of alternatives, noting that the staff were frequently persons weary of the structure imposed by the traditional system. There is little question that the traditional system has been inflexible and less than adaptable to the learning characteristics of all youth, especially those who fail academically and socially.

However, the thinking of the folk heroes of many alternative educators may be reflected in a selection of quotes, drawn together by Gross (1971).

"To a very great degree, school is a place where children learn to be stupid" [Holt]. Paul Goodman "would not give a penny to the present administrators, and would largely dismantle the present school machinery." Jonathan Kozol demonstrates that the schools of one of our major cities destroy the minds and hearts of black children. George Leonard, Peter Marin, and Edgar Friedenberg see schools stifling the finest and most passionate impulses of young people. The high school students who formed the Montgomery County (Maryland) Student Alliance testified that "From what we know to be true as full-time students, it is quite safe to say that the public schools have critically negative and absolutely destructive effects on human beings and their curiosity, natural desire to learn, confidence, individuality, creativity, freedom of thought, and self-respect." (Gross, 1971, p. 23)

15

Gross (1971) made no bones about it. He advocated the radical's platform:

1. Students, not teachers, must be at the center of education.
2. Teaching and learning should stay with the students' real concerns, rather than with artificial disciplines, bureaucratic requirements, or adults' rigid ideas about what children need to learn.
3. The paraphernalia of standard classroom practice should be abolished: mechanical order, silence, tests, grades, lesson plans, hierarchical supervision and administration, homework, and compulsory attendance.
4. Most existing textbooks should be thrown out.
5. Schools should be much smaller and much more responsive to diverse educational needs of parents and children.
6. Certification requirements for teachers should be abolished.
7. All compulsory testing and grading, including intelligence testing and entrance examinations, should be abolished.
8. In all educational institutions supported by tax money or enjoying tax-exempt status, entrance examinations should be abolished.
9. Legal requirements which impede the formation of new schools by independent groups of parents—such as health and safety requirements—should be abolished.
10. The schools' monopoly on education should be broken. The best way to finance education might be to give every consumer a voucher for him to spend on his education as he chooses, instead of increasing allocations to the school authorities. (p. 23)

These statements and the educators who made them are not concerned with evaluation. They seem foreign to most hard-working, system-sensitive secondary educators. Yet, they convey an attitude at one extreme, which may be no more insensitive to evaluation of traditional programs at the other extreme. In short, educators *believe* in things, especially programs. Evaluators *doubt* things both by their nature and because of their job. Educators (believers) tend to be uncomfortable with doubters; therefore, they ignore evaluation as a process. This is not a conclusion, but a speculative assumption that bears further questioning.

COST FACTORS

Oddly enough, administrators have been highly interested in the cost factors of alternative programs. Generally speaking, if the facilities are similar to those of the traditional program, the cost factor is also very similar.

In several cases, alternative programs use community or other cheaper facilities and reduce individual per pupil cost to as much as $700 less than that of the traditional program in the same city (Kenyon, 1979).

PARENTAL EVALUATION

Also oddly enough, a review of evaluative data (Limar & Edmonston, 1976) on alternative programs has demonstrated that the majority of them sample parental opinion. In most cases, the parental attitude is strongly pro alternative education program (Smith, 1973).

ABSENCE OF EVALUATIVE DATA

In this review of alternative program evaluation, few of the therapies or programs that preselect students on the basis of known handicapping condition provided evaluative data. The reason, in part, seems to be related to the administrative organization under which the program falls. If it is a special education program, the chances for evaluation tend to be much higher than if it is a special project.

GENERALITIES ABOUT ALTERNATIVE EDUCATION

Robinson (1973), in the editorial lead-in to the *Phi Delta Kappan's* special issue on alternative schools, said this:

> Although no census report is available, it seems safe to conjecture that a majority of the alternative advocates—at least those working within the system—are not social revolutionaries, but humanistic psychologists who believe that students will learn better in congenial surroundings. (p. 433)

Advocates urge student choice, self-realization, and decision-making. The alternative idea promotes intelligent decision-making by student and teacher; it has not discovered the answer to an effective learning formula.

That is why much of the evaluation dilemma exists. Fantini (1973) and Bremer (1973) said it quite distinctly: Alternative programs are specialized efforts, for specialized audiences, designed to offer a continuum of secondary programs not now available in many secondary schools. It is not their objective to become a replacement for the secondary program, but a continuation of that program. Therefore, the primary difficulty with alternative school evaluation design or procedures at present is that the substantive question is not one of program evaluation, but of construct or concept evaluation. Hickey (1973) clarified the problem when he wrote that the two conflicting demands are (a) the unreasonable rigidity in traditional product-oriented evaluation, which is not applicable to alternative education;

and (b) the view maintained by alternative sensitive educators that their programs "transcend" evaluation.

In evaluating a sociopolitical, economic, and educational construct, at least the following variables *must* be considered:

Community attitude
Staff attitude
Parental attitude
Student attitude
Community participation
Academic achievement
Academic participation
Attendance data
Disciplinary/behavioral data
The extent and nature of feedback
Followup of survey data
Holding power of a program
Changes in student-teacher relationship
Decisions made by the student
Self-concept
Achievement motivation
Development of a preferred learning style
Success in job entry
Success in living.

The list is incomplete, but it represents a few of the variables that affect, and, in turn are affected by, an alternative program. They therefore must be included in the measurement of alternative education. What remains, then, is an absence of evaluation data, especially where specialized students or therapeutic alternative schools are in place. What is so vitally needed is first, a clarity of concept in objectives with criteria; second, a willingness to learn from evaluation data (programmers *must* be believers, evaluators have the right to doubt); and finally, removal of an attitude that evaluation data are final, that they are totally subjective, that good evaluation plans develop no negative findings, and that negative findings mean the program is ineffective. Ineffective as opposed to what? There is no comparative base for most alternative education programs or their students. Therefore, the concept by which a program's objectives are formulated is the only factor at risk. Is not every educational concept generally untried and unproved, open for constructive review? That is all evaluation is. When that fact is accepted, the well-planned, full-time effort by all staff to evaluate may begin. Until then, evaluation of every educational program shall remain at a low ebb—so low, in fact, as to be unusable, and that satisfies those who do not want to be confused by data.

REFERENCES

Bass, G. *A study of alternatives in American education, Vol. I: District policies and the implementation of change.* Washington DC: National Institute of Education, 1978.

Blanchard, R., Knouff, W., & Nelsen, R., *Manual for developing a school-within-a-school alternative program.* Portland OR: Portland Public Schools, 1974.

Bremer, J. Alternatives in education, *Phi Delta Kappan,* 1973, *54,* 449–451.

Cohen, S. A. The fuzziness and the flab: Some solutions to research problems in learning disabilities. *The Journal of Special Education,* 1976, *10,* 129–136.

Coleman, J. *Equality of educational opportunity.* Washington DC: U.S. National Center for Educational Statistics, 1966.

Coleman, J. Class integration—A fundamental break with the past. *Saturday Review,* 1972, 58–59.

Fantini, M. Alternatives within public schools. *Phi Delta Kappan,* 1973, *54,* 444–448.

Gross, R. From innovations to alternatives: A decade of change in education. *Phi Delta Kappan,* 1971, *53,* 22–24.

Havighurst, R. *A profile of the large city high school.* Washington DC: NAASP, 1970.

Hickey, M. Evaluation in alternative education. *NASSP Bulletin,* 1973, *57,* 103–106.

Kenyon, C. B. *ALP: Alternative learning project: Overview of a model high school in Providence, Rhode Island.* Providence: Providence Public Schools, 1979.

Limar, E., & Edmonston, G. P. *Alternative education in Louisiana.* Baton Rouge: Louisiana State Department of Education, 1976.

National Center for Educational Statistics (NCES). *Digest of education statistics.* Washington DC: U.S. Government Printing Office, 1978.

National Schools Public Relations Association (Ed.). *Alternative schools: Pioneering districts create options for students.* Arlington VA: Author, 1972.

Robinson, D. W. Alternative schools: Do they promise system reform? *Phi Delta Kappan,* 1973, *54,* 433–434.

Shanker, A. One man's view. In National Schools Public Relations Association (Ed.), *Alternative schools: Pioneering districts create options for students.* Arlington VA: National Schools Public Relations Association, 1972.

Silberman, C. *Crisis in the classroom.* New York: Random House, 1970.

Simon, R. I., Levin, M. A., Fieldstone, M., & Johnson, A. *The development and evaluation of an alternative high school: A report on SEE. Phase II.* Toronto: Ontario Institute for Studies in Education, 1973.

Smith, V. Alternative public schools: What are they? *NASSP Bulletin,* 1973, *57,* 4–9.

Thompson, E. W., & Shein, H. *The evaluation of the Middle Years Alternative Program, 1978.* Ann Arbor: Ann Arbor Public Schools, Michigan Office of Research and Evaluation, 1978.

Vincenzi, H., & Fishman, R. J. *Impact of alternative programs on an urban school district, 1978.* Presented in a session entitled Longitudinal Designs—in LEA and National Studies at the Annual Conference of the American Educational Research Association, Toronto, Canada, March 27–31, 1978.

Washington, R. A survey-analysis of problems faced by inner-city high school students who have been classified as truants. *High School Journal,* 1973, *56,* 248–257.

CHAPTER 3
Expanded Alternative Program Descriptions

Learning Center II

2366 Eastlake Avenue East
Seattle WA 98102
(206) 343-2340

Darrell Anderson/John Krueger
Program Supervisors

The program is administered jointly by the local education agency (LEA) and the State Juvenile Rehabilitation Division. It serves a multi-district urban and suburban geographic area.

Learning Center II is the smallest of six similar programs operated on basically the same organizational and management model, and serving essentially the same category of client. This particular program serves a client group that is eligible for special education and is funded with monies allocated for the education of handicapped students.

Learning Center II operates under an organization within the LEA known as Interagency Corrections Programs. There is a full-time program manager responsible for this administrative program unit. The business community is involved primarily through the social service agencies that jointly sponsor the programs. The community is involved in like manner, as is the rehabilitation administration. Each of the sponsoring agencies for a particular program has its own internal thrust to reach a specific area of the community. Although the degree of involvement varies, all interagency programs are significantly more involved than most programs operated solely by LEA's. The philosophy behind this system is based on the premise that the development of skills in young people is at the heart of both the educational and social service systems. Hence, a joint focus upon these skills can provide the basis for interdisciplinary learning centers. The educational system serves as the main vehicle for teaching the minimum skills to survive and for delivering agency services.

The primary focus of both agencies is on how well a youth can maintain school adjustment. All other alternatives, such as jobs, additional training, or counseling services, are dealt with after a youth has achieved success in school. School performance is the primary treatment measure.

TARGET POPULATION

The number of youths in the program over a year is approximately 30. Their ages range from 11 to 18, while their grade level is 2.0 to 9.0 depending on the subject area. Typically, grade levels are highest in concrete areas and lowest in abstract areas. The average class size is 10 to 15. The racial balance is generally 50% Caucasian and 50% Black. Classes consist primarily of an all male population.

Handicapping conditions are prevalent. Students exhibit an inability to:

1. Interact productively with peers or adults.
2. Work in a group setting.
3. Discriminate appropriateness of a behavior to a setting.
4. Communicate needs in a manner necessary to have those needs satisfied.
5. Work independently.
6. Complete a task.
7. Attend regularly.
8. Be punctual or keep appointments.

Their overall academic characteristic is a low level of achievement. Previous schooling has been limited to inadequate elementary schooling or institutional schools.

With regard to their socioeconomic level, 50% of the youths have no primary family unit and are in group homes, 20% are living with relatives, and 30% are with their families, but these families are usually extremely dysfunctional. All are of low socioeconomic level and live in inner-city areas.

All of the students have had involvement with the juvenile justice system, and have usually experienced repeated institutionalization. These youths are some of the most disturbed found in an institution, having adjusted minimally and spent considerable time in lockup or security. They are all under parole supervision and have recently been released from an institution. Learning Center II is reserved for the most difficult youths in the Seattle area; they have been suspended repeatedly from all other special and alternative programs. It is often the last available option before long-term incarceration or mental health hospitalization.

CLASS PLACEMENT

For admission criteria, the program directors look for a composite of adjustment problems such as a history of school absenteeism, dysfunctional interpersonal relations, low academic ability, repeated institutionalization with minimal adjustment, current supervision by a correctional agency, and prognosis of failure in any other special education alternative or mainstream school. Referrals come from counselors working for probation, parole, or diversion services.

As soon as students improve their interpersonal functioning they are introduced to a more normal setting on a part-time basis with staff supervision and support. Students are mainstreamed to the next most normal environment when they can show a percentage increase of on-task behavior, school attendance, interpersonal relations, and amount of time spent in school.

Graduation from this school is possible but does not occur since students are moved to a more academic environment as soon as their behavior indicates that they can adapt successfully.

PROGRAM RESOURCES

Professional support consists of one teacher, several juvenile parole counselors, and one parole services specialist. The criteria for selecting teachers is as follows:

1. Diagnostic/prescriptive education training.
2. Behavior management training and experience.
3. Experience in the juvenile justice system.

Every teacher has special education certification. Additional training in behavior management and behavior development has always been necessary. Teachers' salaries are on the same local education agency teacher salary scale.

Staff development takes place in cooperation with the University of Washington. The program takes up the major part of one school psychologist's time, primarily in matters of special education compliance assessment. Social worker support is provided through the functions of the Juvenile Rehabilitation counselors. A non-LEA facility space is provided by the Juvenile Rehabilitation department. Juvenile Rehabilitation provides some program support, equipment, materials, and resources in addition to those the LEA provides.

The educational model focuses both agencies on teaching the skills this type of youth needs for survival in society. Educators and social workers are both involved in a youth's total program; for example, educators attend parole or probation hearings on a youth's behalf, and social workers often tutor in the classroom. By integrating the educational and social service models on a single team that has responsibility for a youth's community program many of the traditional escape routes are closed. An interagency team makes it less likely that a youth will fail either due to system neglect and oversight, or to the youth's own inability to effectively communicate his or her needs.

The payoffs for those involved are significant. Social workers have possibly 5 hours of contact with their clients in which they can observe their day-to-day functioning and have direct and immediate information and impact on their progress. A social worker's expertise can be drawn upon when a youth is first experiencing difficulties and not after expulsion or dropping out of school. School time can also be used to learn how to fill out Division of Vocational Rehabilitation forms, contact employers, obtain public assistance, or appropriately talk on a telephone.

One of the frustrations of educators is having to work without support and without information about the 18 hours a student is not in school. An interagency model supplies extensive background information on abilities, home environment, and other factors affecting a youth's performance. Contact with and impact on those factors becomes easier and is a part of daily educational responsibilities. Support from the social work member of the team allows off-hours handling of contingencies and crises. For example, a social worker may be able to use group home contact to improve attendance, punctuality, or frequency of study.

Youths and their families are able to receive better and more frequent services than before. Not only are they able to draw from more community support systems, but when the family structure is not able to handle a situation, there are two or more professionals able to assist. A family can learn new ways of relating, handling emergencies, and being responsible and accountable.

PROGRAM CONTENT

The goals of the program are to:

1. Provide educational programs in accordance with the criteria for an academic or performance credential.
2. Provide educational and social adjustment learning to direct the students toward re-entry into public or private school programs.
3. Provide general education/basic skills programs in preparation for entrance into independent living.
4. Provide an environment in which students will develop positive social and interpersonal abilities.
5. Provide for the development of the students' ability to undertake independent action and to make free choices within the framework

26

of acceptable standards of conduct established by society.

6. Provide a successful school experience for youths whom no one else is able to work with and who have shown an inability to function in any other environment.

Learning Center II is a day treatment center. Improvement of social behaviors is the primary goal; educational improvement is a treatment technique. The curriculum is focused on basic survival skills and is completely individualized. Emphasis is placed on ability to complete the Seattle Schools Minimum Competency levels of functioning. The program is housed in a formerly unused section of the county detention center; however, the lockup capabilities of the setting are not part of the program.

The program runs for a traditional school year, with summer employment being an option for youths who have shown the ability to handle a structured work situation.

STUDENT MANAGEMENT

Student management techniques are based on the following concepts:

1. Traditional techniques have not worked, so there is constant searching for different methods of management. Most situations are approached from that point of view.
2. These youths suffer from feedback loops that are too infrequent. The staff try to increase that feedback in many different ways, such as daily individual conferencing, group conferencing, weekly "report cards," graphic illustrations, charting of behavior, and reward systems.
3. Failure is success; success is failure. For most of these youths failure is the most familiar school experience they have had and is hence a security. Success is usually highly anxiety-producing. Staff try to wean them from this failure reinforcement cycle. For example, a distinction is made between actual disruptions and those used to reduce success anxiety. The youths are helped to discriminate between the two.

Management and improvement of behaviors is done through any means, exclusive of physical punishment or psychotherapy. Management is a shared responsibility. Day-to-day, on-site supervision of both social service and educational staff is carried out by a social work administrator who is responsible and accountable to both systems. An educational administrator who is not housed in the program manages items of an educational nature that cannot be handled by existing staff. This administrator also helps decide overall program goals and direction. Crisis support is provided by correctional counselors.

PROGRAM EVALUATION

Student progress is indicated through a combination of achievement tests, attendance information, charting of on-task behavior in relation to the amount of time in class, ability to maintain effective interpersonal communications, and ability to work independently and follow through on tasks. Frequent feedback and communication to students in as many different modes as possible are emphasized. Students and their counselors receive information on progress daily, weekly, and monthly in a variety of meetings, conferences, and documents. Anticipation and intervention of problems is facilitated by this process, and it builds a strong team identification. Daily information is summarized, and the results are given to the students, parents, and parole/probation counselors through individual meetings and by mail. Feedback about on-task ability and appropriateness of behavior is given daily to the students and their parole or probation counselors. Specific behaviors are targeted by agreement of counselors, teachers, and students. Amount of time in school, amount of time on-task, behavioral interventions, and major events are tracked and the results are reviewed periodically with the students and their parole counselors.

Grades are too emotionally laden to be easily handled by these youths. Progress is noted by pointing out changes in skill levels. Credits and grades leading to graduation are meaningless in the sense that completion of school is not a realistic goal for these students. Staying out of institutions, earning a living, and increasing their belief in themselves are realistic goals.

The most valuable factors in being able to conduct such a nontraditional program have been staff support and the co-funding from the state juvenile corrections system. During the 4 years the program has been in effect no student has ever been suspended or expelled. While youths have been returned for short institutional stays, management supports the use of all options to keep this from happening and build successful experiences.

PROGRAM FUNDING

The program is funded cooperatively under two basic sources: some reallocation of state juvenile rehabilitation monies and state handicapped monies. Learning Center II itself receives no grants from the two sources mentioned; however, other units within the interagency program area, while not receiving funds for the handicapped, do receive either some categorical support from the state or an extra measure of the basic education funding used throughout the local education agency. To date, social service has provided the facility, transportation, counseling, and site management. Teachers, curriculum, teaching aides, management, and reintegration services have been school district supported. Services to out-of-district students are billed to the responsible LEA through the standard interdistrict contract. The costs for a student at Learning Center II are two and one-half times as expensive as for a regular basic education student.

Bellefaire School

22001 Fairmount Blvd.
Cleveland OH 27013
(216) 932-2800

Vince Julian, Principal
Ronald P. Weitzner, Assistant Principal/Supervisor

Bellefaire School is an integral part of the Bellefaire Residential Treatment Center. It is also an official public school serving adolescent youth in the Cleveland Heights/University Heights school district. The school was inaugurated in 1953 as a part of the Cleveland Heights/University Heights school system. Throughout the year, the Bellefaire School, as well as the residential treatment center, has served children throughout the United States and Canada, although more specifically it is a mid-west regional center and emphasizes local placements in the greater Cleveland area. In addition to its in-town 32-acre campus, Bellefaire has a 60-acre camp in Pierpont, Ohio. The camp facility is used extensively as an integral part of Bellefaire's treatment program.

The faculty participate in the governance of the program by serving on various review boards that meet regularly. There are 12 review boards evaluating all aspects of the school program. The Policy Review Board has the primary responsibility of directing the other 11 boards. The review boards focus on such areas as behavior, placement, vocational training, and assessment. These ongoing committees allow the teacher to act as a member of the decision-making team. Bellefaire is accredited by the Joint Commission on Accreditation of Hospitals as a Psychiatric Facility, by the American Association of Psychiatric Services for Children, and by the Child Welfare League of America.

TARGET POPULATION

Bellefaire serves approximately 100 students, both boys and girls, ranging in age from 8 to 18. The median age is 14. The students are severely behaviorally handicapped as well as multiply handicapped, severely behaviorally handicapped/educable mentally retarded and learning disabled/behaviorally handicapped. Forty are welfare cases. The academic abilities of the students are widely divergent. Generally speaking, their intelligence levels are average to above average; there are a few who have low IQ scores and several in the gifted range. A large number of the students are dyslexic in one or more areas.

Some of the students have been involved in the juvenile justice system, usually because of minor infractions of the law. Children treated at Bellefaire usually have incapacitating neurotic or character problems with serious failure of functioning within the family, the school, or the community. They come from all types of public and private school backgrounds. The full range of socioeconomic levels is represented, from welfare populations to families from some of the finest suburban areas. The student population is primarily Caucasian, with about 10% Black. Half of the students are Jewish, and the other half are Gentile. The school serves students from the residential portion of the Center as well as the day treatment, group homes, and those students who only attend Bellefaire for the educational offering and return home in the evening without any other involvement at the Treatment Center.

CLASS PLACEMENT

Fire setters and students on hard drugs are not accepted. A multi-factored assessment provides the social, psychological, and educational data necessary to place students in an appropriate program. Much of this information is compiled by the sending agency or school district. Students remain in the program for approximately 2 years. They are referred by the courts, parents, psychologists, child guidance clinics, teachers, mental hospitals, and other social agencies. The intake study by the clinical staff includes a professional assessment of the child's disturbance as well as areas of strength. There is an emphasis on developmental, social, and academic history as well as current adjustment. Psychiatric, psychological, and medical information is reviewed, as is the quality of family and peer relationships. Following preliminary review of material, the family visits Bellefaire to become acquainted with the program and to enable the agency to enhance its knowledge of the child. Families are able to participate in mutual goal-setting.

Approximately 20 students are mainstreamed on a part-time basis into the Cleveland Heights/University Heights school system. Bellefaire School has followup placement. Staff help the student make the transition from the institution to the community. Data are collected on how well the students rate in the educational program. Because of the relationship of the Bellefaire School with the Cleveland Heights High School system, students are able to receive the same diploma upon graduation. Students can graduate from Bellefaire as opposed to being mainstreamed. After-care services for children who remain in Cleveland include casework and special education. Local and regional children who must move gradually from Bellefaire's protected environment to living in the community may be placed in one of five group homes, an adolescent group residence, or an individual foster home, all of which are supervised by the Jewish Children's Bureau, an affiliate of Bellefaire. Out-of-town children are often referred to agencies in their home communities for after-care services.

PROGRAM RESOURCES

Student-teacher ratios vary with the levels concept at Bellefaire. Level I, the most restrictive classroom, has a student-teacher ratio of 6 to 1. Level II represents the majority of students and has a ratio of 8 to 1. Level III, the community-bound program, has a ratio of 10 to 1.

The school has 16 SBH (Severely Behaviorally Handicapped) units and two vocational instructors, OWE and OWA (Occupational Work Experience and Occupational Work Adjustment). The other staff consist of a full-time occupational therapist, a career consultant, one full-time reading consultant, one half-time reading teacher, a full-time substitute, a school monitor, and a crisis interventionist who deals with suspensions and emergencies. Supplementing this staff are a corps of 30 volunteers from the community who serve as teacher aides. All of the teachers are certified in LD/BD and were hired through the Cleveland Heights/University Heights Board of Education. Each student is supported by a treatment team composed of the teacher, case worker, child care staff, treatment team leader, and unit social worker. In addition to mainstreaming students into the Cleveland Heights/University Heights system, services can be purchased from Cleveland Heights in order to enrich program offerings. The teachers have the same salary scale as the regular public school teachers with an additional $300 differential for teaching students in special education. Teachers also have the option of working in the summer program for additional reimbursement. The summer program is 6 weeks in duration and is sponsored by Bellefaire. Help and cooperation are received from the United Way, the Jewish Community Federation, 648 Board, and many other agencies and organizations in the community.

The Bellefaire School works closely with John Carroll University. A grant from the Martha Holden Jennings Foundation, jointly administered by John Carroll University and the Bellefaire School, has been used to develop an on-site training program for prospective teachers of students with behavior difficulties. In an attempt to narrow the gap between practice and theory, a number of Bellefaire faculty have served as lecture consultants at John Carroll, while John Carroll faculty have held courses on-site at Bellefaire. Prospective teachers serve internships at Bellefaire School's unique 6-week summer session. Bellefaire also serves as a training facility for student teachers from Kent State University throughout the school year.

PROGRAM CONTENT

The treatment program at Bellefaire is an integrated program of group living, education, and psychotherapy designed to meet the unique needs of each child and family.

Group Living

Each of Bellefaire's eight cottages accommodates 12 to 14 children. These small units ensure individualization and maintain the intimacy of a small treatment unit within the overall Bellefaire program. The unit supervisor, child care workers, and psychiatric consultant plan a therapeutic milieu program designed to foster the growth and development of each child as well as the group.

Education

The Bellefaire School, in session 11 months of the year, is organized on an ungraded basis and provides an individual curriculum for each child. Teachers are selected jointly by Bellefaire and the Board of Education.

Psychotherapy

Individual, group, and family psychotherapy are the predominant methods of psychotherapy used at Bellefaire. The amount and type of psychotherapy are determined according to the needs of the child and family. Some children are treated with psychoanalysis by one of the child analysts on the treatment staff.

School is in session from 8:30 a.m. to 2:30 p.m. daily. The day treatment program extends until 5:30 p.m., with a Saturday program also included. Students and residents return to group living after school. All students receive individual psychotherapy and are directed in recreational and skill activities. After school hours, psychiatric case workers work with local parents.

Once a year, as the individualized education plans are being completed, parent conferences are held to discuss the child's school program for the coming year. The teacher and the educational supervisor analyze each student's academic strengths and weaknesses and then prescribe a program designed to correct disabilities as well as to reinforce existing skills. Both long-term and short-term goals are tailored to the individual child and include academic as well as prevocational curricula. Program objectives include helping the student to:

1. Develop a realistic self-image as a worthy human being who is able to contribute to his or her growth and the growth of others.
2. Master and regularize daily living skills and meet social expectations.
3. Master the impulsive aspects of behavior (acting-out or constriction).
4. Identify appropriate personal goals and learn a problem-solving process as a means of pursuing personal goals.
5. Master the skills necessary to optimally pursue educational/vocational goals.
6. Relate and communicate with adults in a constructive give-and-take relationship, recognizing the authority of adults without loss of his or her own autonomy.
7. Relate to peers in a constructive, give-and-take relationship and derive satisfaction from group involvement and activity.
8. Invest in and derive satisfaction from community activities.
9. Become prepared for eventual transfer into a community public school.
10. Receive vocational training if he or she is not academically oriented.
11. Be provided with counseling and direction in the areas of career awareness, values clarification, and character building.

STUDENT MANAGEMENT

A unique aspect of Bellefaire is the "Step Upward Approach." Students are placed in class based on levels of behavioral competence rather than academic competence. The levels concept is divided into two tracks—academic and vocational. Students progress upward as they develop greater inner controls and assume more responsibility for their behavior. The program also attempts to match teacher styles and treatment theories to the students' behavioral level.

The first level is *activity-oriented*, where students learn fundamentals and, more importantly, learn to succeed. "Transitional" students attend one of four classes in buildings outside of the regular school. The staff utilizes team teaching and behavior management techniques in both academic and prevocational activities to build confidence in each student and to replace fear of failure with a series of successes. Emphasis is placed on survival skills, hands-on experience, and an academic point system.

Level II, the *open school,* places the student in the Bellefaire School. In this setting, attention is focused on individualized instruction either in vocational or academic areas. The vocational track is guided by OWA (Occupational Work Adjustment) for students who are 14 and 15 years old. The OWA student has classroom instruction in job attitudes, job skills, and career planning. During the remainder of the day, the student works at campus jobs for which he or she is reimbursed.

At the open school, all Bellefaire students can take advantage of the many special programs offered. Students are scheduled for academic and skill seminars consisting of photography, electronics, gym, math tutoring, music, shop careers, and human potential courses.

In Level III, *community-bound,* the student begins to spend part of each day in one of the surrounding school districts. Approximately 20 students attend classes in public schools throughout Cleveland Heights and other suburban districts. These community-bound students have worked their way to the highest level and are capable of functioning well in the public school or in an off-campus work experience. The OWE (Occupational Work Experience) program guides students 16 years and older in this area. At this phase, the academic-bound or vocational-bound student realizes the greatest degree of self-actualization, and he or she is given the most opportunity to assume responsibility.

The Level IV phase deals with *followup* and *placement* of the students who have left Bellefaire during the past year. The role of the Followup Coordinator is to help students during this difficult transitional period between institutional and community living. Counseling and guidance are offered students as they seek to find jobs or continue their education in the community. They are also helped with financial matters as well as survival skills. Information is obtained from Level IV students in order to evaluate the school's effectiveness.

Bellefaire strongly believes in preventive measures and promotes an elaborate recognition system consisting of commendation cards, principal's lunch club, student-of-the month, student-of-the year, and honors banquet. However, when behavior problems do occur, the teachers have an elaborate support system to rely on after they have exhausted all of the following interventions:

1. The school monitor provides life-space interviewing and time out.
2. The crisis intervention staff member supervises in-house suspensions.
3. If the student does not respond to these, there is a behavior review board made up of faculty and administration who develop behavior contracts with students who are having difficulty with their management.
4. The next intervention is to send the student to the placement review board, where a determination is made regarding a change in class placement or a drop from one level to another.

When all these approaches fail, school personnel meet with the total treatment team to develop good strategies or consider discharge. The Bellefaire School also has a student leadership corps. Staff and administration work very closely with these students in order to obtain their support in behavior problems that occur in the school such as vandalism or smoke breaks.

Finally, perhaps the most effective behavior management technique at Bellefaire is the levels concept, where students are placed in a particular level according to their behavior readiness. Teachers are then matched to these particular levels according to the teacher's personality, philosophy, and behavior style. The levels concept deals with the emotional, behavioral, developmental, and academic needs of the students by employing a matching concept. Level I is primarily behavioristic, Level II is directive, and Level III is facilitative.

Level I

Behavioristic intervention features a highly structured classroom. This is the most restrictive approach and should be used for students who are lacking in inner controls. It emphasizes the shaping of behavior through systematic utilization of contingencies.

Level II

Directive intervention is for students who have gained limited degrees of cognitive control and whose daily behavioral choices are reasonably responsible. The interventions that are emphasized include Glasser's Reality Therapy, Dreikurs' Adlerian Psychology, and Redl's Naturalistic Approach. The teacher using directive interventions usually develops a contractual arrangement regarding behavioral expectations agreed upon mutually with the student.

Level III

Facilitative intervention employs aspects of Rogerian Psychology and Ellis' Rationale Emotive therapy. This approach is employed with the students who are developmentally the most inner-directed and who possess the highest cognitive control of the Bellefaire School population.

All of the teaching staff should be familiar with and comfortable in employing each of the psychoeducational approaches. On any given day, a particular student may need to be assisted by the use of a variety of interventions. However, in developing this mode, it has been discovered that most of the students can be developmentally or functionally identified as benefitting more overall from one approach than another. Thus, a levels system has been developed matching student characteristics with teacher style and educational objectives representing the most profitable learning arrangement. An accurate blending of desired objectives, teacher style, and the student's developmental/behavioral level allows the "Step Upward Approach" to follow this matching model as shown in Table 2.

TABLE 2
Levels System

	Objectives	*Teacher style*	*Student's developmental/ behavioral level*
Level I	Extinction of disruptive behavior; establishment of basic inner controls.	Direct, dominant, authoritarian— implements behavior modification techniques.	Little or no control over behavior; frequent acting-out episodes; some bizarre behaviors.
Level II	Increased inner controls; maintenance of desirable behaviors; beginning development of interpersonal skills.	Blend of direct and indirect, democratic and authoritarian— uses reality therapy techniques and behavior modification techniques as appropriate.	Inner controls established, but need reinforcement; needs to maintain age-appropriate behavior and learn social and academic skills.
Level III	Preparation of student to return to community; firmly established inner controls.	Indirect, reflective, democratic— implements reality techniques, aids and reinforces decision-making by the student.	Inner controls well established; needs to develop self-confidence and increase interpersonal and academic skills.

PROGRAM EVALUATION

Students receive weekly status reports from their teachers. Report cards are issued every 9 weeks. Grades are given students from 9th grade through 12th grade. As a part of the levels concept, Level IV represents followup in placement. Students are interviewed several weeks prior to discharge, and they provide detailed information regarding the strengths and weaknesses of the school program. One of our staff serves as a part-time liaison person to help students make a smooth transition from institutional life to a role in the community. The 12 review boards monitor every aspect of the school program, including such areas as behavior placement, policy, and recognition, so that on an ongoing basis staff are constantly evaluating and making adjustment to the program. One of the main objectives at Bellefaire School is to mainstream students into the community for jobs as well as for academic programming. At the present, an average of 20 students per year are mainstreamed into a public school setting. Approximately 15 students have off-campus jobs. Factors contributing to the success of the "Step Upward Approach" are as follows:

1. Stability of the teaching staff.
2 Relationship with the public school system, the school being an integral part of the residential treatment program.
3. The behavior levels concept.
4. The matching of teacher's style and personality with the developmental needs of students.
5. The recognition system.
6. Individualized creative instruction.
7. Career specialist.
8. Biweekly inservice and support system to teachers.

PROGRAM FUNDING

Because of Bellefaire's relationship with Cleveland Heights/University Heights in being considered a part of the public school system, Bellefaire is eligible for state funding. It is presently being funded for 16 SBH units as well as two vocational units. Additionally, a portion of the SBH supervisor's salary is reimbursed by the state.

Bellefaire currently has a grant from a private foundation called the Jennings Educational Foundation, which is helping to train teachers who will work with SBH students. The school receives funds from United Way as well as the Jewish Federation, and the per student expenditure at the Bellefaire School is approximately $3,400. That is the excess cost figure for tuition in the school, compared with approximately a $2,000 figure for regular students attending Cleveland Heights/University Heights schools.

Longfellow Education Center

3017 East 31st Street
Minneapolis MN 55406
(612) 729-7358

Robert W. McCauley, Director
Jodie A. Erikson, Educational Coordinator

The program was established and opened to formal referrals and students in June, 1979. Longfellow Education Center (LEC) is administered under a special contract to #916 Special Intermediate School District from the Twin Cities Area Educational Cooperative Service Unit (ECSU), which receives funds through a grant from the Minnesota State Department of Education, Federal Projects Office. The geographic area served includes the seven-county metropolitan Twin Cities region—49 school districts, including St. Paul and Minneapolis. The region includes inner-city, suburban, and exurban (semirural) areas.

TARGET POPULATION

The Longfellow Education Center is designed to serve multiply handicapped youth who exhibit serious emotional disturbance. It was established to serve 60 seriously emotionally disturbed adolescents, ages 11 to 16 and grades 6 through 9. The average class size is 10 students. Of the 60 students, 82% are White, and 18% are Black, Native American, or Hispanic.

The primary handicapping condition is serious emotional disturbance or severe behavior disorder. However, children have also been diagnosed as learning disabled, educable mentally retarded, language disordered, and neurologically impaired. One child is also blind; a second has experienced a serious case of encephalitis.

Students' academic characteristics are heterogeneous—individually and as a group. Each student can present a range of characteristics—such as the very poor reader who has exceptional knowledge of science concepts. Typically, the students range from the lower five percentile ranks to the upper percentile ranks (90%) in reading, mathematics, language arts (spelling, writing, expression), language and speech, and general junior high school curriculum subjects. Approximately one-third of the students have been classified as learning disabled, language deficient, or educable mentally retarded in the past.

Students' behavioral characteristics are heterogeneous but can be clustered under the general description used by the Longfellow Education Center program, which states: "The child exhibits a pattern of development, behavior, and learning over a significant period of time and with sufficient intensity such that:

1. "Persistent problems are present in general learning or classroom behaviors": for example, the student plays truant–out of and in school; is inattentive to directions, tasks, and performance expectations; does not complete assigned tasks; does not accept changes in routine; is verbally abusive; is physically threatening or abusive; refuses to comply with basic school safety rules; does not utilize choice or leisure-recreation time positively; requires continuous supervision by staff; or does not correlate behavior, feelings, and consequences.

2. "Satisfactory interpersonal relationships and interactions with peers, home, or other significant adults (e.g., teachers) are generally lacking": for example, the individual has no friends or associates with problem behavior peers. Negative interactions occur frequently. The student does not find relationships a source of support, motivation, or reinforcement.

3. "Perceptions or descriptions of self are consistently expressed as negative, derogatory, inadequate, or not in concert with family or school expectations": for example, the student calls himself or herself names, and does not believe that she or he can achieve, make progress, or develop positively.

4. "Learning or achievement is below home and school expectations, or is variable from school term to school term or year to year": for example, the student has generalized deficits in academic skills or makes minimal progress in basic academic skill areas or general curricular areas.

5. "General pervasive moods of anxiety, depression, unhappiness, or withdrawal from interactions are present": for example, the student trembles, cries, twitches, or hyperventilates when in behavioral or emotional crisis.

6. "Physical illnesses or fears are associated with personal or school problems": for example, the student engages in excessive absenteeism; exhibits phobic reactions to specific situations; or frequently wants to be sent home from school due to illness.

Students have received a wide range of special education service prior to placement at Longfellow. The third area of placement criteria is "Prior Service," that is, the insistence that students have had at least part-time special services for a significant period of time that have proved unsuccessful. Most often, students have been in self-contained classes, programs, or schools prior to LEC placement; have a history of tutorial or management aide service; or have been in residential, hospital, or correctional programs prior to placement.

No specific indexes of socioeconomic status are collected on students. The range of socioeconomic status apparently is from poor urban and suburban youth (working and welfare families) to wealthier urban and suburban families (professional and management employment families). Of students in the program, 70% are from single parent, foster parent, or group home situations; 40% are from families that have known histories of alcohol or drug abuse; and 40% are from families in which apparent or known instances of child abuse have occurred.

Approximately 50 to 60% of LEC students have been involved with the juvenile justice system. The primary reasons have been for community offenses such as breaking and entering, home problems such as running away, school problems such as truancy, or LEC problems such as assault on a staff member. Placement is *not* due to involvement in the juvenile system, however. Often, involvement with that system is a correlate of other life problems being experienced by the child.

CLASS PLACEMENT

The six-step identification, referral, and placement process is designed as a collaborative decision-making process. The parents, the child, the local school district, and LEC are all participants in the decision-making process. Each step is designed so as to help all participants determine whether or not to proceed to the next step. The process can be continued or terminated by any participant's informed consent at any step. Furthermore, the process is designed to ensure parents' (and children's) civil rights.

Since LEC is a metropolitan regional program and many sources could potentially refer students (e.g., local education agencies, courts, welfare services, parochial school district), all referrals must be made through the student's current local school district and signed off by the local Director of Special Education. All persons who have worked with a referred student can submit data relative to the referral to LEC, but only the school district can actually conduct the referral. Furthermore, only the local school district is responsible for tuition, billing, and transportation of a student placed at LEC.

Once a student has been placed at LEC, attempts to integrate the student with nonhandicapped children occur primarily after school hours and outside the school setting. LEC is a self-contained, 100% special education day placement. Significant attempts are made to maintain the child in home-community activities and programs such as social clubs, sport teams, recreational groups, and peer support groups.

As a child progresses through the program, she or he is moved into the Transition Program. This phase is designed to integrate the students into a less restrictive educational placement in his or her local district (or other appropriate district). Transition emphasizes integration by placing a child in a vocational assessment and job tryout program, part-time attendance in the less restrictive educational program, and more integration into community events or programs.

Students are intially placed in LEC for 1 school year or less. Major individualized education program revisions and evaluations of the placement occur at 6-month intervals. A student potentially could be enrolled at age 11 and dismissed at age 16 (LEC's upper age limit), but the general criterion is that a child must show substantial progress in order to remain beyond a 2-year period. Lack of progress is seen as a mismatch between the services of the LEC program and the child's needs, and more appropriate educational programs would be sought.

Children typically are enrolled for 1 to 2 academic years. Progress is determined by the achievement of specified objectives in the areas of Routine Management, Reinforcement, Social Behavior, and Academic Skills. These are labels for areas that spell out expectations relative to management of self around school routine, to acceptance of consequences correlated with behavior, to appropriate and positive interactions and relationships, and to increased performance on school tasks and curricula.

Of course, realities of age determine student graduation; youngsters who reach age 16 leave even though they may not have accomplished all objectives. Also, students move out of the program due to other, out-of-school problems such as arrests in the community, parents suddenly moving outside the metropolitan region, or parents refusal to continue placement in the next school year.

Transition from the LEC occurs most often to the local education district and involves a combination of programming components. Many students return to a blend of regular school programming (junior or senior high level); special education support or resource program instruction; work-study or vocational education programming; and/or support counseling from peer groups, counselors, therapists, or community-based child counseling programs (e.g., youth counseling services available through community juvenile correctional systems or chemical dependency peer support groups). Transition occurs 1 to 3 months prior to actual dismissal from LEC, on a part-time or full-time basis in the local school program. Consultative assistance is provided to the new program, primarily by the LEC Liaison Teacher.

PROGRAM RESOURCES

Personnel

To accomplish program objectives and serve 60 students, LEC employs the following personnel: a director, an educational services coordinator, six classroom teachers of the emotionally disturbed, a crisis teacher, a learning disabilities teacher, an adaptive physical education teacher, a liaison teacher, a psychiatric nurse, a social worker, twelve program assistants, and other instructional or consultative support as necessary. The pupil-teacher ratio is 10 to 1.

All teachers must have appropriate state licensure or be able to obtain license variance or a provisional license from the state. Unlicensed staff (those on variance or with a provisional license) must obtain the appropriate license within 1 or 2 years through completion of a state-approved, university-based training program. Salary is determined by negotiated contract with the #916 Special Intermediate School District. No variation exists for special education versus other types of teachers.

Staff are hired after an exhaustive interview and evaluation process. In keeping with good professional practice, legal requirements and regulations, and affirmative action procedures, interviews adhere to knowledge and competence required for a job and specified in job descriptions.

PROGRAM CONTENT

The program's goals are four in number:

1. To provide appropriate psychoeducational diagnostic services to suspected unserved and underserved severely emotionally disturbed youth residing within the Twin Cities Metropolitan region.

2. To provide an intensive, daily educational program (self-contained) to unserved, underserved, and more restrictively placed youth (ages 11 to 16) who are severely emotionally disturbed or

have multiple handicaps of which severe emotional disturbance is the primary handicap.

3. To maximize each student's opportunity for re-entry into a more normalized (less restrictive) setting by providing training and demonstration to the student's resident district staff; stimulating local or subregional program alternatives for students requiring less intensive special education services by providing consultative assistance; and providing training opportunities for representatives of all interested local educational agencies (LEA's).

4. To provide behavioral management training, family support, and referral services and family counseling services as indicated by the student's and family's needs.

In order to accomplish these goals over a period of 3 years, the Longfellow Education Center is comprised of three basic components: evaluation and education, outreach, and family service.

Evaluation and Education Component

An individualized diagnostic and treatment planning service is made available to appropriately referred children. These services involve assessments of intellectual, educational, emotional, social, medical, neurological, and sensori-motor functioning of individual children and interactive assessments and plans relative to the match between individual children's needs and environmental factors and components. During the referral process, the Longfellow Education Center relies on assessment information and reports available from the LEA and other persons and agencies. Further evaluations are conducted as a supplement as needed. Within the LEC program, progress assessments are made by the continuous collection of classroom performance data and more formal periodic evaluations.

A daily educational program is provided to severely emotionally disturbed children who may best be served in a self-contained environment designed according to validated child development and learning principles. Such principles are implemented through systematically arranged instructional programs that facilitate child progress toward prescribed goals. Children enter the program into a self-contained class unit (Level I in LEC parlance) and, as they are behaviorally ready, move into curriculum structures calling for greater amounts of self-management, responsibility, and a lessening of structure and supervision (Levels II and III). Children received classroom instruction, resource program instruction, adapted physical education, crisis support, art and exploratory education, and prevocational curricula as part of the general services offered by the program.

Outreach Component

A teacher education program and consultative assistance to districts is being developed for individual, small-group, and district- or agency-wide use. The major purposes of these efforts will be to (a) maximize individual children's successful re-entry into more normalized educational, community, and life settings; (b) disseminate valid programming components and strategies for emotionally disturbed children; (c) enhance participating districts' and agencies' services for disturbed children; and (d) preclude the inappropriate exiting of mildly to moderately disturbed children from local district placements to more restrictive settings.

Outreach services are intended primarily to provide service to LEA's that have enrolled students in the Longfellow program. However, districts and service agencies requesting or requiring the development of professional performance skills to serve disturbed youth also may receive inservice education.

Family Service Component

Services to families of LEC students are provided through a variety of program offerings and relationships designed to support family change and growth in coping with the emotionally disturbed adolescent. Behavior management training, cooperative home-school relationships and contracting, joint IEP planning and development, family counseling and referral, and mutual home-school recreational activities are available. LEC personnel are required to have frequent and supportive interactions with students' families, and parents or guardians are consistently encouraged to interact with the LEC.

Daily Educational Service

The major component established thus far is the daily educational service. As noted before, the program is a 100% self-contained day program for emotionally disturbed young adolescents. The program is provided as an alternative to residential placement and as a potentially appropriate placement for children exiting from other special settings. The program operates during the traditional academic year (September to June) and provides a 6-week, half-day permissive (or optional) summer program. Children are transported to the school through arrangements made by the local school district, ordinarily on a bus, van, taxi, or public bus, from their current living situations—the family home for 95% of the residents, with a community-located group home situation in effect for 5% of the students.

47

The curriculum offerings of the LEC range from basic skills to junior high level courses. The majority of students need continued development in reading, mathematics, spelling and writing, and language skills. Most students fall below the 40th percentile on normative evaluation instruments and indicate scattered or deficient basic academic skills on criterion- or curriculum-referenced assessment instruments. Furthermore, many students are lagging in general knowledge areas (e.g., social studies, literature, language arts, sciences, music, art), language concepts and usage, study skills, independent learning skills, and the ability to generally meet the varied expectations held for secondary school students.

However, a large group of students are sufficiently skilled in basic academic skills that they need the ordinarily available junior high curriculum. Thus, curricula such as literature, algebra, history, political processes, and music and art are provided. Physical education is provided to all students, ranging from a 1 to 1 movement and motor development skill session to large group classes ($N = 10$–12).

All curriculum offerings are related to the IEP goals and objectives prepared for each student. When a child's special needs are related to basic academic skills and classroom responses, his or her curriculum program is slanted in that direction. A modification in emphasis occurs for students possessing intact basic academic skills. Whichever emphasis is given in the student's curriculum, the IEP acts as a guide and working document to determine instructional tactics, responses or skills to be sought, and achievements to be measured.

Many students receive individualized instruction for a large portion of the day, especially if instruction is focused on the attainment of basic skills. However, group instructional arrangements are employed with students as frequently as possible. For reasons of both social and cognitive gains, the LEC program approximates the typical junior high as much as possible, stressing cooperative group-oriented methods and making progress in a group context.

Direct teaching strategies are implemented as the program develops. Direct teaching strategies are those derived from a task analytic or behavioral learning formulation. Simply stated, instructional and curriculum approaches are based on valid learning principles and concepts. These strategies emphasize a structured use of time on-task; the acceleration of accurate and proficient responses; frequent reinforcement of student performance; modification of teaching and curriculum according to student performance; use of sequenced materials, tasks, or skills; deceleration of error responses or nonresponding; continuous monitoring of student progress; implementation of effective classroom management procedures; and use of support services in direct work with students. The LEC is highly interested in the application of learning principles in its program for gains in both social and cognitive domains.

STUDENT MANAGEMENT

The Longfellow program attempts to use comprehensive approaches to student behavior development as well as management. The LEC views the primary responsibility of special education to be the development of new behaviors and strengthening of present behaviors that facilitate positive, productive interactions and commitments with peers, parents, communities, and professionals. To respond to this responsibility the Center attempts to organize management systems that incorporate effective behavior development and management strategies into sequenced interventions, especially using less restrictive interventions.

Behavior development and management procedures can be organized under two basic approaches: positive programming strategies and behavior interference strategies.

Positive Programming Strategies

Positive programming strategies emphasize the development of (a) new behaviors; (b) social skills; (c) affective education, encouragement, and support; (d) prevention of disruptive behavior; (e) focus on behaviors to be strengthened; (f) individualized goal setting; (g) group interactions, norm development, and problem solving; (h) relationship development; and (i) self-management and personal responsibility.

Behavior Interference Strategies

Behavior interference strategies emphasize the decrease of (a) generally disruptive classroom behaviors; (b) verbal abuse, manipulation, or negatives; (c) property abuse or destruction; (d) physical threat, attack, or assault; (e) negative and nonproductive interactions with peers, teachers, parents, and community; (f) self-derogation or consequences; (h) refusal to complete or noncompletion of assigned class work; and (i) behaviors preventing acceptance of greater amounts of self-regulation and responsibility.

Since it would be difficult to thoroughly describe every behavior development and management procedure used, the following sections describe general approaches used at Longfellow.

First, behavior development is often sought through group intervention strategies. Each homeroom class begins the day with a goal-setting and problem-solving group during which students select, review, or seek feedback on a social goal and academic goal. Students often select a daily academic goal and weekly social goal. These goals

49

help students develop a sense of commitment or motivation for progress, assist in specifying immediate behaviors to be developed, and frequently (90% of the time) seek positive interactions or gains with students.

At the end of the day, a group meeting is held again. The teacher reviews the goals with students, seeks and encourages feedback on goals, and determines which students have accomplished their goals for that day. This achievement is recorded, either on a student's contract or in some other form. Appropriate points or reinforcers are awarded at that time.

Many teachers also use group-based reinforcement strategies with their instructional groups. This usually is a classroom-wide token economy system. As students engage in behaviors related to task accomplishment, meeting social interaction expectations, and self-management gains, they earn points that can be used for purchasing products, special events, free time, recreational activities, out-of-school field trips, relationship time, and so on. Token economies emphasize positive, approving social interactions, especially reinforcing naturally occurring social interactions. Each group token system is different, yet focuses on the essential group expectations found within a classroom: being on time, finishing on time, having materials ready, knowing and working on one's goals, being helpful to others, participating in group lessons, avoiding removal from the group and so on.

Classrooms themselves are grouped according to a "levels system," and each level holds a somewhat different group focus. There are three levels of classrooms at the LEC:

Level I. *Entry classroom.* The focus is on individualized academic instruction, behavior development and management, intensively structured programs, and basic self-management. As progress occurs, more side-by-side (parallel) group work is sought, increased emphasis is placed on beginning interaction skills, and higher expectations for self-management are held.

Level II. *Advanced classroom.* The focus is on small and large group academic instruction, behavior development and management, and higher expectations for self-management and development. Classrooms are oriented more toward cooperative interactions, learning group relationship skills, and age-appropriate (junior high) academic performance.

Level III. *Transition classroom.* The focus is on large group academic instruction; age-appropriate behavior development and management; expectations to self-regulate most parts of school, home, and community life; and separation from the

50

program to local district or other appropriate, less restrictive programs. Classroom structure is diminished to general expectations of a junior high school classroom, and heavy emphasis is placed on cooperative, responsible socialization skills and interactions.

Each student has a "code" status related to basic school privileges. Students can change codes through their behavior. A summary of code privileges is shown in Table 3.

TABLE 3
Summary of Code Privileges

	Code A	Code C	Code E
Student:	1. Reports to classroom in morning from bus. No free time.	1. Reports to classroom in morning from bus. Has free time in room.	1. Chooses where to be before school (outside, class, recreation room).
	2. Is escorted by staff between classes and in building. No hall passes.	2. Goes to classes and moves through building on hall passes.	2. Manages own schedule. Does not need hall passes.
	3. No morning break in recreation room.	3. Has morning break in recreation room.	3. Can negotiate break times.
	4. No out-of-school field trips.	4. Can go on scheduled field trips.	4. Can work with teachers to plan field trips or independent study.
	5. No computer terminal time.	5. Can use earned free time. Can work on computer terminal.	5. Can become computer terminal key operator.

Each student begins on Code C when enrolled in the program and remains on Code C until he or she either is dropped to Code A for specific behavior problems or contracts to move to Code E.

A drop to Code A occurs automatically for the following behaviors: (a) physical assault, (b) excessive verbal abuse, (c) use or possession of drugs, (d) running away from the program, (e) truancy, and (f) being caught smoking.

51

A student is on Code A for the rest of that school day and through the next day. If no further violations of code behavior occur, then the student automatically returns to Code C.

To earn Code E, the student negotiates a contract with the teacher for a minimum of 10 school days. The contract includes an agreement to maintain Code C for that period and to attain at least four individual behavioral goals during that time. Furthermore, the student must agree to develop a Code E "maintenance contract" once he or she has achieved Code E.

Another basic approach to behavior development used extensively at the LEC is *contracting*. A variety of contracts are established between teachers and children, related most often to goals, codes, level changes, and/or classroom token economies. In order to assist in setting goals, receiving feedback, earning points, and so on, new students are given an entry contract when they begin at LEC. This contract lasts for 2 school weeks, and is either renegotiated for a third week or is concluded. The student then negotiates a specific, individualized contract, lasting for a specified period and related to behavioral goals to be achieved. Contracts are most often related to levels goals, code changes, and IEP objectives.

Crisis management occurs through the implementation of crisis and time-out plans for each student. School district policy is to implement an "aversive-deprivation program" for any youngster who is placed in out-of-class time out, is physically restrained, or is removed from his or her generally available instructional situation twice during a month. The aversive-deprivation program is developed in conjunction with a positive behavior development program, and is intended to decrease self-abusive, assaultive, destructive, or dangerous behaviors. Any aversive-deprivation program must be documented as needed, be reviewed by both the Child Study Team and a building Review Team; be established as an IEP revision requiring parent permission; and be carefully implemented, monitored, and evaluated.

Within the LEC, a Crisis Team has been established to aid the program to (a) prevent crises where possible, (b) interrupt crises so as to restructure a student's emotions or behavior, and (c) engage in post-crisis counseling where appropriate. This team meets at least weekly to review students who enter time-out procedures or experience other forms of crisis and to determine who would likely be effective in working with crisis-prone students. Much of the work of team members is oriented to direct teaching or counseling of students in how to avoid or decrease recurring crisis situations.

The LEC also has a Crisis Teacher, whose role is to assist students and staff when they enter a crisis and to conduct time-out procedures when necessary. The time-out procedure is designed to systematically present a series of more restrictive consequences to students engaging in specified disruptive behaviors.

PROGRAM EVALUATION

Student progress is determined primarily through the systematic, continuous collection of observational data relative to student behavior. LEC uses a levels system to provide measures of progress. Student behavior is observed and rated daily and summarized weekly for behavior development objectives within four goal areas. These objectives are, in turn, related to individualized objectives in the annual IEP. As a student consistently achieves his or her objectives, decisions are made as to whether or not to move the youngster to a different level.

Other measures of progress are to monitor academic achievement. When a student enters the program, he or she is ordinarily assessed with normative instrumentation in the general areas of reading, mathematics, and general information and assessed through criterion- or curriculum-referenced instruments so that instruction may be instituted at an appropriate level. Frequent measures of mastery are taken to determine whether or not a child is accurately and proficiently mastering prescribed curricula.

Finally, goal attainment and maintenance are monitored through analysis of contracts, point accumulations, and periodic reviews of IEP's. Oftentimes, graphs are prepared displaying point totals and goal attainment as feedback to students and staff.

Grades are not given at the LEC. However, frequent progress reports on specific goals are sent home to parents. Also, accomplishments and achievements are converted into credits when they are needed in a home school district. Such conversions are often needed for youngsters entering 10th grade.

The program is now in its second full year of operation. Little data relative to overall program achievement have been collected. A need to develop that data base is acknowledged.

PROGRAM FUNDING

The Longfellow Education Center is currently funded through a mixture of Public Law 94–142 discretionary dollars that go to the Minnesota State Department of Education and local school district special education formula allowance and transportation money. Longfellow was established as a project by a State Department Discretionary Grant, funded from state-received P.L. 94–142 dollars. The local school districts who use the program pay transportation costs, which are reimbursable in part from state aids and the allowable formula aid as "tuition." Thus, 80% of the Center's budget is derived from federal dollars and 20% from local dollars and state aid.

As the Center develops, it will shift from federal-state discretionary money to local funding sources. In essence, the Longfellow budget will gradually (over 2 to 3 years) change to local dollars for which state special education reimbursement aids are available and will charge tuition for that portion of a child's educational program not covered by reimbursements.

The Metropolitan Twin Cities Area ECSU conducts all billings to districts served. The billing occurs twice annually and is based on the number of days during which the student was enrolled. Separate billings occur for summer school.

SPRING
(Special People Realizing Individual New Goals)

892 Vedado Way, N.E.
Atlanta GA 30308
(404) 875-7704

Peyton Towns, Director

Georgia has 24 psychoeducational centers, geographically distributed to serve approximately 160 school districts. The target population comprises severely emotionally disturbed individuals. Up until the school year 1979–1980, the psychoeducational network served children only up to the age of 14.

SPRING was founded in October, 1976, with the first objective being to develop a model for serving severely emotionally disturbed children over the age of 14. The second and third objectives, respectively, were to orient agencies, schools, and decision makers to the needs of these youngsters (basically a lobbying effort) and to serve a limited number of severely emotionally disturbed adolescents and their families.

Initially, SPRING served only students in the Atlanta Public School System. Decision makers eventually recognized the need to serve severely emotionally disturbed children over the age of 14, and, when these funds were allocated, SPRING expanded services to three other school systems. In addition, the other psychoeducational centers were allocated funds to begin serving severely emotionally disturbed adolescents, and the SPRING model was recommended for adoption and adaptation on a state-wide basis.

SPRING is administered by North Metro Children's Center, one of the 24 psychoeducational centers. North Metro Children's Center, in turn, is administered by a board consisting of the four school superintendents from the four school systems it serves.

The school systems are the Atlanta Public School System, Fulton County School System, Gwinnett County School System, and Buford City Schools. The population served includes inner-city, suburban, and rural. SPRING has three sites, one serving primarily inner-city Black youngsters, one serving primarily white-collar White, and one serving primarily blue-collar White children.

TARGET POPULATION

SPRING serves approximately 150 students during a school year, mainly between the ages of 15 and 18 and in grades 8 through 12. Team teaching is employed to a great extent. The average class size is 1 to 10, and each class has an aide.

Nearly 50% of the youngsters served are schizophrenic, with a few autistic-like children and one totally autistic child. The rest have a variety of diagnoses, primarily "unsocialized" and "socialized aggressive." Approximately one-third of the SPRING students are involved in the juvenile justice system, but the typical SPRING student is more likely to be involved in the mental health system. Academic levels range from first grade to college levels, and IQ's range from the retarded to the very gifted. One girl has an IQ over 150.

CLASS PLACEMENT

Referrals are received from schools, hospitals, various professionals, parents, courts, Department of Family and Children's Services, and other agencies. Depending on the school system, either referrals are channeled through the school system or at least the system is made aware of referrals. After a referral is received, significant sources such as parents, schools, and other agencies are contacted to gather preliminary information. A screening is held to determine whether or not the referral looks appropriate enough to proceed with the intake process. If so, a psychological test is administered, a home visit is made, and a family psychosocial history is taken. In addition, information from schools and other agencies is gathered. A due process staffing is held to determine whether SPRING can best meet the objectives of the individualized education program (IEP) and whether, consequently, it is the most appropriate placement for the student.

The determination of whether an adolescent is truly emotionally disturbed or behavior-disordered, and not socially maladjusted, delinquent, or culturally different from the dominant society in his value system, is a complex problem. Stated simply, the question is whether the student is in pain, and therefore motivated to change, or whether it is his environment that is in pain. Project SPRING has concluded that it is better to use clinical judgment and individual evaluation instead of adhering to a broad, rigid classification system that may exclude students who should be included and include students who should be excluded. Information relative to the adolescent's problems—and necessary for determination of emotional disturbance—is obtained through psychological evaluation, which includes personality and projective testing; a social case history, including family history, symptom picture, and mental status; and information obtained from other agencies.

An additional tool for determining emotional disturbance is the Quay classification system for behavior-disordered adolescents. Two instruments, the Behavior Problem Checklist (Quay & Peterson, 1979) and the Behavior Checklist for the Analysis of Problem Behaviors from Life History Records (Quay, 1967) discriminate five categories: unsocialized aggressive, personality disorder, immature-inadequate disorder, subcultural delinquent, and psychotic disorder. These instruments are not used as the sole criteria for determining placement, but they do yield valuable information and provide help in determining placement.

Various combinations of the following provide criteria for placement:

1. Psychiatric and/or psychological evaluation of (a) severe depression, (b) phobic reaction, (c) chronic severe anxiety, (d) psychosis (either borderline or stabilized through ongoing psychiatric treatment), and (e) other classifications (except that of character disorder or severe organic retardation).
2. Significant high scores on the Quay instruments in the dimensions of personality disorder, immature-inadequate disorder, or psychotic disorder.
3. Extremely poor or nonexistent peer relationships.
4. Impingement on all areas of the adolescent's life.
5. Inability to behave as society expects, as opposed to *unwillingness* to behave as society expects.
6. Long-term chronological adjustment to the dominant society's values and patterns, with very recent onset of *severe* disruption in relationships with authorities. Behavior is the result of an underlying psychological problem and not solely a power struggle between the adolescent and significant authorities in his or her life.

Discharge or termination in the program is based on two types of criteria: definitive and evaluative.

Definitive Criteria for Discharge

These criteria include the following:

1. The student is mainstreamed fully to regular class placement.
2. The student is mainstreamed to a specific job training program.
3. The student is mainstreamed to full-time employment
4. The student is mainstreamed to a less restrictive alternative program.
5. The student graduates.
6. The student moves out of area.

Evaluative Criteria for Discharge

At times students should be terminated for reasons other than the above such as chronic truancy, institutionalization, or failure to respond to psychoeducational treatment. In such cases, the Project staff must rely on individual evaluation and good clinical judgment to make a decision. This can be difficult; however, it is the Project Director's responsibility to ensure that the program is providing the maximum services possible. If a student is attending only once a month, he or she is probably not getting the benefits of treatment that another student could be receiving.

Some variables the staff need to examine in cases of truancy include (a) reasons the student gives for nonattendance, (b) cooperation of the parents, (c) control the parents still have over the adolescent, (d) the student's previous record of attendance (he or she may be going through a crisis), (e) court involvement with the student, (f) the student's age, and (g) the student's activities while not in school. In cases of institutionalization, the main variables to examine are location of the placement and estimated length of institutionalization.

One last idea should be mentioned regarding termination, and that is final evaluation. Exactly what is success? If the student lost the job he was working on or decided to drop out of the program he was in, and did not want to come back to Project SPRING, has the school failed? After all, he is not being productive. Although the student has better survival skills such as being able to read, communicate better, deal with authorities better, or perhaps most importantly, he has more confidence in himself and his ability to deal with his problems in society without hurting others or himself, the fact remains that he still is not paying taxes. Should this be listed as a failure?

Not really. It is not easy to determine, but if that individual is less of a burden on society than he seemed destined to become, the apparent failure is, in reality, a success. The student may now be able to get a certain job if he decides, because he can read the application form. Or he may now realize that a boss is a boss regardless of whether he is right or wrong, and an employee must act accordingly. He may be able to keep his psychotic thinking to himself and his therapist, or realize that he has some control over his depression and can, with help, maintain himself outside of an institution.

Few college students have chosen a career by the time they graduate and seldom do they make a lifetime career out of the first job they take. It seems unreasonable to expect a severely emotionally disturbed adolescent, who is developmentally far behind the nonhandicapped population and is burdened with a multitude of other problems, to suddenly become a normal, stable, productive, taxpaying citizen. Vocational counseling and planning have very high priority within the Project SPRING treatment format, but they are not the only goals for treatment. Indeed, the question may be not what a severely emotionally disturbed adolescent can do for society during his lifetime, but whether or not he can live within that society.

PROGRAM RESOURCES

The program staff consists of eight teachers, eight aides, three treatment facilitators (site lead teachers), four social workers, one psychologist, a consulting psychiatrist, two secretaries, and a director. The teacher/pupil ratio is approximately 1 to 10 and the teachers have special education certification or provisional special education certification. Their salary is comparable to that of regular education teachers, and staff development activities are scheduled often, many being in cooperation with nearby universities. The program relies somewhat on support personnel in the local schools, depending on the local schools' resources and the relationships developed with those schools.

Perhaps the most unique equipment the program utilizes is the motivational equipment found in the student lounges. Each site has a student lounge where the students may relax, play pool, or listen to music if the right is earned.

The program has a variety of relationships with various agencies in the community. Some agencies provide enormous support and cooperation, while others do not. It has been the experience of the staff that agency support and coordination is usually best achieved on a person-to-person basis rather than on an agency-to-agency administrative basis. In other words, the social worker does not call up X mental health center, but calls up Miss Jones at X mental health center.

For the first 2½ years the parents were very involved in keeping the project alive. The project was scheduled to be defunded on five occasions. The parents rallied and wrote letters to the school superintendents, school board members, legislature, and governor. They held a legislative open house and became very involved in seeing that the project continued. Had it not been for the parents of Project SPRING, there is serious doubt that the psychoeducational network would now be serving severely emotionally disturbed children over the age of 14.

In addition, parents are involved in a variety of PTA activities such as dinners on holidays, field trips, and fund-raising activities for field trips. From time to time, parent counseling groups and education groups are held, and some parents are in actual family therapy with program staff.

Philosophy

The SPRING model makes the assumption by definition that education is the transmission of survival skills of a culture and of its individual members to the progeny of that culture. This is the purpose and process of education. If the culture in question is an Indian tribe, the skills that would be important to teach are greatly different from those of modern Western civilization. It may be important to teach an Australian Aborigine child how to hunt, make clothes from animal hides, or live in the outback for 6 months alone. However, in terms of survival skills needed in modern America, it is much more important to learn how to read, write, and manipulate numbers. For most Americans, being able to locate jobs, arrive on time for work, and get along with the boss or other coworkers are more important skills for survival than knowing how to farm or hunt.

Psychoeducation of the emotionally disturbed child is similarly seen as transmitting survival skills of our culture. However, because of the nature of the population, the survival skills that are considered important are somewhat different from those of conventional education. Reading, writing, and arithmetic are considered important, but reducing socially inappropriate behavior or psychological pathology and increasing communication and socialization skills are just as important, if not more so. For this reason, the disciplines of psychology and psychiatry are relied upon to teach such survival skills in an educational framework. Using this definition of education, psychotherapy itself can be seen as a special type of education in that the therapist is attempting to teach the client how to cope successfully with his or her problems. Within this context, the purpose of psychoeducational treatment utilizing the SPRING model is to teach emotionally disturbed adolescents how to survive in society outside of institutions and, hopefully, to make a contribution themselves to that society.

60

PROGRAM CONTENT

The major components of this model include a curriculum, a motivational system, and a management system or systematic method of setting limits. Included within this model is an emphasis on group and individual counseling, with techniques developed for that counseling; an Outreach component serving adolescents not appropriate for the day treatment program; and a system for close staff and parent communication. One other effective aspect of the model is that the Project is part of a comprehensive high school, yet is managed by a psychoeducational center. This allows the flexibility necessary to program for severely emotionally disturbed adolescents, yet it provides maximum impetus toward successful mainstreaming as the students are stabilized.

SPRING can best be described as a school within a school, with some students being self-contained and others being mainstreamed for most of the day. The program is in session during the traditional school day, although afternoon and night field trips are offered quite frequently. Most students live at home or in foster homes, while a few live in group home situations. Transportation is provided by the local school districts.

The academic and vocational curricula are individualized, with some students working on remedial reading and mathematics, some students studying for the G.E.D., and others focusing primarily on prevocational skills or working on a regular curriculum. IEP's are written for each student, with parental input and student input as appropriate.

Day Treatment Program

If it is determined that the student is appropriate for the day treatment program, he or she is placed in the orientation phase for 10 to 15 school days. During this period the student is exposed to all aspects of the program and is evaluated in terms of academic skills, behavior, vocational adjustment, and family relationships. After this period, a total service plan (TSP) is drawn up consisting of long-range goals in any or all of these four areas. The student and family are requested to give maximum input into this process and are called in to discuss and sign the finished product. In addition, an IEP is drawn up at this time, consisting of short-term methods and goals with estimated dates of completion. The IEP is the means to reach the completion of the total service plan, with every goal on the TSP having a corresponding IEP drawn up. At this time, an individual counselor is chosen with

61

whom the student must spend at least 30 minutes a week in a private counseling session.

In a typical school day for students who are in the self-contained program the students are in individual academic instruction for approximately 3 hours in the morning; after this, there is lunch and a break in the student lounge for those who have earned it. Daily group counseling, an afternoon activity such as field trips, arts, crafts, and physical education follow. The students who are mainstreamed into regular high school classes move in and out of that schedule.

There are two levels of group counseling. One is citizenship, a structured, didactic group consisting of students whose poor reality testing, immaturity, or lack of self-esteem prohibit them from extensive, constructive encounters. Student interaction and encounter are encouraged; however, when a discipline problem begins to develop or a situation is arising that is too intense for the more fragile members of the group, the leader can structure the group back to the task at hand. The second group is the advanced group and is a much less structured encounter situation involving techniques taken from a variety of therapies including Reality Therapy, Gestalt Therapy, and Relationship Therapy. The group leader will always have a task or "ice-breaker" in mind for the group, but the emphasis in the advanced group is on process, as opposed to the more product-oriented emphasis of the citizenship group.

Outreach

In addition to the day treatment program, there is an Outreach component. There are three types of students to be served in this aspect of the program. One is the student whom Project SPRING is trying to bring into the center but who is unable or unwilling because of depression, phobia, or other factors. The second type is the student who is already in school or on the job for whom our objective is maintenance and support. The third category of students to be served in Outreach consists of those for whom we feel another program is more appropriate at this time, and our objective is to get them there. For example, if the student is primarily a socially maladjusted delinquent, we may try to get him into a street academy. If he is severely psychotic or dangerous to himself or others, we may try to get him into a hospital and stabilized, after which we may serve him in the day treatment program. Services provided in Outreach include on-site academic evaluation and tutoring, survival competency training, individual and parent counseling, coordinating referrals and followup to other agencies and programs, vocational counseling and evaluation, referral for specific job training, or further vocational evaluation and possible job placement.

Parent Services

Cooperation and support from parents are actively solicited from the moment the student is referred. Theoretically, parent services are based on the Karnes model and include behavior management training, parent counseling, parent groups, and referral for social services. The major foci of parent services have tended to be problem-solving and goal-setting contacts. Whether the problem is with the student in school, at home, or in the community, close parent communication is essential to a student's success with the program. It should be noted that the parent services keep the student as the focus. For marital or family counseling per se the family is referred to a mental health center.

Goals of Instruction

In summary, the goals for students at Project SPRING are as follows:

1. To live in the community, not in institutions.
2. To be responsible and regular in attendance.
3. To learn basic survival skills including the 3 R's, prevocational and vocational skills; to live with authorities; to develop relationships with peers; and to establish goals.
4. To become mainstreamed to regular education, specific job training, or job placement.

STUDENT MANAGEMENT

Basically, the key in managing the behavior of disruptive adolescents (such as acting out or truancy) is to motivate them to participate successfully in the program. Authority figures such as parents or probation officers enhance the motivational component of the program; however, a conscious effort is made to establish a motivational component within the program itself. This component consists of three aspects. One is the obvious "hooker," such as the student lounge, pool table, breaks, or field trips. Second is the involvement the student develops with the staff and other students. The third aspect is "structuring for success." Staff expect and ask students to do only what it is obvious they can do. When the motivational component is intact, the management system becomes a reality and the student can be exposed to the desired curriculum.

The student is initially on a token system, in which he or she must earn all of the possible tokens each period in order to participate in breaks and go on field trips. Also in effect is a response cost (reinforcement) procedure, which is basically a systematic way of consequating behavior and setting limits. There is a policy and procedure the staff use in implementing response cost, with sensitivity, objectivity, and fairness being an integral part of the process. The essence of this system is that by accepting the staff's authority and following rules, the student is exposed to the positively reinforcing activities of the program. This can just as validly be seen as a punishment procedure, for if the student refuses to accept the staff's authority and follow rules he or she is not permitted exposure to these activities. However, the Project SPRING model prefers to focus on the idea of increasing acceptable behaviors, as opposed to decreasing unacceptable behaviors, and therefore defines response cost as a negative reinforcement procedure.

If a student can come to school 15 days in a row, with no unexcused absences or tardiness, and earns all of his or her tokens at the appropriate time, he or she can move off of the token system and is said to be on the Response Cost Level. On this level, the student is *expected* to follow the routine, obey staff, complete assignments, and participate appropriately. In return, all activities and breaks are given, as opposed to being earned through tokens. In addition, the student is allowed more privileges. It should be noted that the response cost system is still in effect, and continuous inappropriate behavior will place the student back on the token system.

The idea is to move the student from an externally planned, controlled, and directed environment with constant feedback to an internally directed and controlled orientation with natural feedback coming from successful accomplishments and meaningful relationships. It is felt that the latter system is much less artificial in comparison to a regular high school or work situation, and successful re-entry into a normal environment is much more likely. People do not get tokens for driving within the speed limit, but breaking the limit can cost.

In summary, the management system is conceptualized as having three stages: (a) prevention of discipline problems, (b) limit setting (by the front-line worker), and (c) follow-through (when a counselor/administrator must get involved). A staff member can assign a consequence (Stage II) for unacceptable behavior at any time. The student will not be allowed to participate in the motivational component (e.g., breaks, field trips) until that consequence is completed. If the student defies that staff member (e.g., goes on break anyway), the chief disciplinarian must get involved (Stage III). In a regular high school situation, this is usually described as "being sent to the principal's office."

Students are constantly involved in punishment decisions and procedures. One can hear, "It's your choice; I can't make you do it" frequently at Project SPRING; however, that statement is followed up with, "But you know what the consequence is."

In terms of crisis support, the program works closely with hospitals, courts, and other agencies, depending on the student and who is working with the student.

PROGRAM EVALUATION

Students are rated daily on various factors such as appropriate interaction with staff, appropriate interaction with students, general program appropriateness, mood, anxiety, and target behavior. In addition, a brief narrative is included on the record. In the classroom, a record is kept of tokens earned and of students who have moved off the token system on good days. If a student has too many bad days, then he or she moves back to the token system.

All day treatment staff are involved in daily graphic charting of therapeutic activities of the day. The charting consists of three components:

1. A Likert Scale, 1 to 9, of four constants: (a) increase in target behavior, (b) appropriate interaction with peers, (c) appropriate interaction with adults—cooperation, and (d) general program appropriateness.
2. A three-degree rating scale of two variables: (a) mood and (b) anxiety.
3. A narrative to provide: (a) a daily incident report, (b) personal conference summaries, (c) type and extent of behavioral consequences, and (d) a weekly summary.

The assignment of the charting schedule is made by the Educational Coordinator. The actual charting is kept on master weekly graph sheets located in the main files and completed at 3:15 p.m. each day. At 8:10 a.m. the following day, the treatment staff meets for reporting on the previous day's charting and the addition of information to the charts by other treatment staff. During reporting, the Educational Coordinator records daily significant summaries of each student, located in the main office. The previous week's charting graphs are turned in to the secretary by 3:10 p.m. each Monday for filing in students' IEP folders, also located in the main files.

The number of regular high school courses a student can take is another indication of success. Grades are given, and Project SPRING students are in competition with regular education students; however, a student far behind in grade level would get credit for remedial math, not geometry. High school credit is based on attendance, with three instances of tardiness equaling an absence. Promotion is based on credit earned.

Nearly 50% of the SPRING students are mainstreamed for at least one regular high school course. A student can remain in the program until graduation or until fully mainstreamed. When a student approaches completion of his or her total service plan, a re-entry checklist is designed for the student's specific situation. This checklist includes steps involved in the gradual re-entry of the student into the projected environment and the establishment of long-range goals the student would like to realize on his or her own, as well as the working through of termination feelings the student may hold for the group, staff, or individual counselor. Also included in this re-entry process is time for the staff to work through their feelings regarding termination. Students are followed up after exit, and attempts are made to get them involved in vocational rehabilitation, other agencies, technical schools, colleges, or actual job placement. Two SPRING graduates are currently in college.

The Research and Development Department of the Atlanta Public School System has been responsible for evaluating Project SPRING. An evaluation of the previously identified critical variables done in January, 1978, indicates a substantial degree of success. Out of 23 children whose attendance was calculated and whose previous attendance was poor to nonexistent, 7 had 100% attendance after referral, 7 had 90% or better attendance after referral, 6 had 80% or better attendance after referral, and 3 had less than 80% attendance after referral. In addition, on the average of every 5.6 months in the program, each student made 14.2 months growth in math, 16.7 months growth in reading comprehension, and 11.2 months growth in reading recognition.

In terms of evaluating the initial project's first and second goals, namely, developing a model and lobbying for services for severely disturbed adolescents, the program has been successful. Factors that have contributed to the success of the program include (a) hiring the right personnel, (b) keeping the lines of communication open among staff, (c) reducing bureaucratic hassle for staff, and (d) selling the program to anyone who would listen. One other way to measure success is by identifying a definite need, meeting that need, and making decision makers aware of the process.

The major pitfall to success was probably the severity of the population served; however, that probably turned out to be an asset rather than a liability. When the program would take a youngster nobody else wanted or would deal with and, in many cases, make some positive changes in that youngster, the program's reputation was greatly enhanced.

PROGRAM FUNDING

The project began with a federal VIB Grant. Staff have been assigned to the program from the Atlanta Public School System, the Fulton

County School System, and the Gwinnett County School System. Currently, the program is funded by approximately one-half federal discretionary Public Law 94–142 dollars and approximately one-half state dollars.

There are no billing procedures for the students. The program is funded on a year-to-year basis at no cost to the students or families. The per student expenditure is approximately $3,100 per year, compared to approximately $1,800 for a regular student.

REFERENCES

Quay, Herbert, & Peterson, Donald. *Behavior problem checklist.* New Brunswick NJ: Rutgers State University, 1979.

Quay, Herbert. *Behavior checklist for the analysis of problem behaviors from life history records.* Miami, FL: Univ. of Miami, 1967.

CHAPTER 4
Brief Alternative Program Descriptions

SAIL Project
(Student Advocates Inspire Learning)
Special Education Support Service
for Dropout-Prone Adolescents

Chas. A. Lindbergh Senior High
Hopkins School District #270
2400 Lindbergh Drive
Minnetonka MN 55343
(612) 933-9356

Mary J. Balfour, Director

SAIL was established in September, 1976. It was funded for the first 3 years by ESEA Title IV-C funds with state special education reimbursement, and for the last 2 years by local and state funds. The project is administered by local school district Hopkins #270, which serves a middle-class suburban area west of Minneapolis. The project is housed in a resource area within Lindbergh High School. All students live at home and use regular bus transportation within the traditional school day.

SAIL is a total systems model of intervention designed to help students cope academically, socially, and emotionally in an integrated school environment.

TARGET POPULATION

SAIL serves an average of 100 students in a given school year, with approximately 60 students served at any one time. These students range in age from 14 to 21 and are students in grades 10, 11, and 12 at Lindbergh High School. Staff work with students on a one-to-one basis and in groups (approximately 8 to 11 students) three times a week. They are almost exclusively White, English-speaking, and middle class. All of these students are initially identified as dropout-prone. They are assessed and labeled as emotionally disturbed students. They

71

exhibit numerous behavior problems, are often involved in the juvenile justice system, and have had significant experience with loss and victimization.

Most of the students also experience problems in one or more of the following areas: legal infractions, chemical and alcohol abuse or dependency, physical abuse, sexual abuse, serious family disturbances, authority conflicts, dysfunctional peer relationships, and psychological problems. They display an inability to learn that cannot be explained by intellectual, sensory, or health factors, and they have a tendency to develop physical symptoms or fears associated with personal or school problems.

CLASS PLACEMENT

Students are referred to SAIL by teachers, administrators, and parents through the regular special education child study process. Referrals are based on three specific criteria:

1. The student is a former dropout who wishes to re-enter school.
2. The student is strongly considering dropping out of school soon.
3. The student is functioning as an "in-school dropout." That is, the student is failing to earn a minimum amount of academic credits due to excessive absences or chronic failure to complete assignments.

After the Child Study Assessment has been completed and students have been recommended to receive special education service, the student and family have an opportunity to discuss the placement recommendation and the reasons for the referral with school representatives.

SAIL students are in mainstream classes. They can remain in the program until they graduate, although there are different levels of service. Some leave after achieving a satisfactory grade point average for a certain period of time. Services end with high school graduation.

PROGRAM RESOURCES

SAIL constitutes one of Lindbergh High School's support services. The project staff also includes one psychologist, one social worker, three learning disability teachers, one chemical dependency counselor, and one teacher for the educable mentally retarded. They are certified and hold degrees in education, special education, social work, or psychology. SAIL staff serve as case managers and advocates for the family.

Subjective criteria include: (a) experience with schools; (b) experience with adolescents; (c) experience in counseling, both one-to-one and group; and (d) sensitivity, warmth, flexibility, maturity, and assertiveness. The ratio is 15 students to 1 staff person.

Parents are involved in intake, program planning, and review. They are contacted at least biweekly—usually by telephone, but sometimes in a conference or by note. Their involvement varies greatly.

The SAIL staff also encourage students and their families to use appropriate community resources if needed, including chemical/alcoholism treatment programs, court services, state employment services, medical clinics, and counseling agencies.

PROGRAM CONTENT

Basic assumptions of the SAIL program are as follows:

1. A systems interpretation and treatment approach is most effective.
2. Change is possible.
3. Students are responsible for their own behavior.
4. The search for villains is not productive. Significant adults in the child's life have done the best they could at the time.
5. Accountability is essential—by students, parents, and staff.
6. Open communication between all facets of the system is crucial—students, parents, faculty, administrators, community agency personnel, and SAIL staff.
7. Dropout-prone students need intensive counseling assistance. Modified curriculum and work experience programs are useful, but only tangential, remedies for the students' core problems.
8. School is the best place for most youth.

All students in SAIL are completely mainstreamed and participate in the regular high school curricula and are heterogeneously grouped in academic classes. In addition, SAIL students participate in intensive group sessions with SAIL staff 3 days a week for 1½ hours per day. Each student also meets with a SAIL staff person for an individual session weekly. In addition, SAIL staff confer weekly with each student's classroom teachers for reciprocal sharing of information regarding the student's academic progress.

The core methodology of Project SAIL is Goal Attainment Scaling. This goal-setting process is used in SAIL as the student's individualized education program (IEP), the focus of treatment, communicating about the student's progress to parents, and as a method for evaluating total program outcomes. Goal Attainment Scaling is a goal-setting process that encourages individuals to set concrete, measurable goals that are realistically attainable. Staff assist students to select 6 to 15 individualized goals with at least one goal related to attendance and

73

academic achievement in each class. Additional goals mutually negotiated by the student and staff relate to problem areas such as ag-
gression, dependency, chemical abuse, hostility, passivity, suicide,
responsibility, sexuality, peer relationships, authority conflicts, or delinquency. Students are also expected to select at least one goal focused on maintenance of a currently successful area of functioning or
personal strength.

Students score these goals each Friday in their group, and discussion focuses on mutual recognition for goal attainment. This provides
a vehicle for immediate and continuous feedback for the student
regarding ongoing progress. At the end of each 9-week quarter, an
overall goal attainment score is calculated for each student. Students
can receive elective credit for participation in SAIL; however, this
credit is contingent upon successful attainment of at least half of the
goals.

STUDENT MANAGEMENT

Most self-management teaching takes place in the one-to-one and
group counseling sessions. Other behavior management techniques
include negotiations with peer support, make-up time, and contracts.
Specific policies exist for such areas as attendance and chemical/
alcohol use.

Attendance in SAIL Group

1. Students are expected to attend all group sessions, one-to-one conferences, and parent conferences.
2. Each absence requires make-up in the SAIL area or as negotiated.
3. SAIL meets four times per week. A student will not receive SAIL
credit if he or she misses seven times each quarter.
4. Contracts will be negotiated individually in extreme cases.
5. If at the end of the quarter the student needs to make up for
absences, she or he will receive an Incomplete, which must be made
up within 3 weeks into the next quarter.

Chemical/Alcohol Use

1. Students are expected to remain drug/alcohol-free during the entire school day. When a student is observed using or possessing
drugs or alcohol of any kind, the regular school policy will be in
effect: referral to Dean of Students, notification of police liaison

officer, automatic out-of-school suspension for 3 days, and finally a parent conference to be held before re-entering school.

2. When SAIL staff perceive that a student smells of liquor or marijuana, the following steps will be taken: (a) SAIL staff will contact the student's parents and the Dean of Students; and (b) the student will be sent home for the day, and his or her teachers will be informed regarding this absence.

PROGRAM EVALUATION

Students receive a Pass grade for SAIL if they meet one-half of their goals and meet SAIL attendance requirements. This is an elective credit that can be used to fulfill graduation requirements.

The SAIL program has proven to be a successful method of intervention with this high-risk population and, most importantly, it has shown that emotionally troubled, dropout-prone youth can experience success in the regular academic setting without being segregated into a self-contained, mini-school environment.

During the first 2 years of SAIL, 75% of SAIL students who were in the project 2 or more quarters achieved their individual goals relating to academic achievement and social/emotional development. Of the students who were in SAIL two or more quarters, 71% did not drop out of school. Of the students who did not drop out, 79% earned at least the minimum number of credits.

PROGRAM FUNDING

From 1976 to 1979 ESEA Title IV-C and state special education reimbursement funded SAIL. From 1979 to 1980 ESEA Title IV-C support was granted only for a half-time dissemination consultant. Direct service was provided by local (30%) and state (70%) special education funds.

The current per student expenditure is approximately $695. The cost of the SAIL program for each student is comparable to any Level III special education program.

In March, 1979, SAIL became a validated state project, allowing other Minnesota school districts to apply for replication funds through ESEA Title IV-C. The amount of these funds is typically 10% of the third year ESEA funds.

The Starr Commonwealth Schools Alternative Education Program

RR #2, Box 84
Van Wert OH 45891
(419) 238-4051

James R. Beard, Director

Established in 1978 and administered by The Starr Commonwealth Schools in cooperation with the Van Wert County Juvenile Court and the Van Wert County Local School Districts, The Starr Commonwealth Alternative Education Program (AEP) represents a unique cooperative effort between public and private agencies. The program is located at Van Wert, a city of 12,000 in a predominantly rural county of northwestern Ohio. The school is situated on a wooded 40-acre country estate and has an atmosphere similar to a small private boarding school. The program operates on an 11-month academic calendar, although counseling services are provided to students and families for the entire year.

The Starr Commonwealth Schools serve troubled children and their families from several states in the Midwest, with campuses in Albion, Michigan; Van Wert, Ohio; and Columbus, Ohio. As a comprehensive children's organization, Starr Commonwealth provides alternative day school programs, family and child guidance clinics, and residential programs for emotionally and socially maladjusted children. Starr Commonwealth is a nonprofit agency governed by a voluntary board of community leaders and is supported primarily by purchase of service funds from referral agencies and contributions from individuals and foundations.

TARGET POPULATION

Male and female students ages 14 to 18 who have a need for behavioral remediation, value re-orientation, and academic remediation are served. The alternative school provides a self-contained individualized program for 10 students and shares facilities with the residential treatment program of The Starr Commonweath Schools.

Reflecting the socioeconomic composition of the county, the program predominantly serves White lower to middle class youth. Students generally exhibit inadequate academic progress; personal, family, and social adjustment problems; and juvenile and school code violations. A wide range of behaviors such as nonachievement, school and home truancy, severe authority conflicts, drug abuse, vandalism, and other delinquent offenses are exhibited by students.

Students entering the Alternative Education Program (AEP) have been involved in the mainstream educational system prior to entrance in the program. Before consideration is made for entrance into AEP, students have been exposed to a range of in-school options in order to correct their problems. This program is viewed as an alternative in the continuum of services lying between regular school placement and residential treatment.

CLASS PLACEMENT

Students must voluntarily elect this placement, and admission is determined subject to the development of an individualized education program. The admission process utilizes the resources of court personnel, public school teachers, the parents, and school support personnel such as psychologists and social workers. The steps in the referral process include:

1. Initial contact with the Juvenile Court.
2. Determination by the Juvenile Court as to whether or not the student is an appropriate candidate for AEP.
3. Consultation with officials from the Juvenile Court, the public school, and the parents and youth involved.

The process is viewed as a cooperative effort between the school, the court, the parents, and the alternative school staff. While enrolled in AEP, youths may continue to participate in extracurricular activities. However, in order to achieve maximum benefit from this intensive program, most youths spend the entire academic day in an integrated social-behavioral-educational experience. The intent is to provide the maximum impact in the minimum amount of time, so that a student can be returned to the regular setting as soon as possible.

Students may enter or leave the program at any time during the year, although a youth is not ordinarily enrolled for more than a year. "Graduation" is granted according to the youth's progress in achieving behavioral and academic goals.

The re-entry process into the school system involves a very extensive commitment on the part of the alternative school staff. Throughout the child's stay, the staff work closely with parents, school, and court personnel to determine those problems that need to be resolved in order for the student to return. At the time of graduation from AEP, groundwork has been established for a smooth and successful re-entry into the public school.

PROGRAM RESOURCES

Key program staff include a special education teacher, an educateur, and a part-time secretary-aide. Starr Commonwealth's residential program provides administrative coordination for AEP as well as the availability of a resource teacher. Consequently, there is a ratio of approximately 3 staff members to 10 students. All staff in AEP are trained in the educateur concept. Educateurs work directly with children and their families in a variety of living/learning environments. While cognizant of the problems of exceptional children, the educateur's focus is not on pathology but on the child's potential for normal behavior and development (Heward & Orlansky, 1980).

The difference between the educateur's work and that of the psychologist, psychiatrist, or social worker is that the former takes place in all parts of the child's everyday activity, contrasted to the other forms of help, which often take place outside of normal life and reality. Educateurs are trained in special education and therapeutic recreation as well as the behavioral sciences, and are certified in the area of behavioral disorders (Brendtro, 1980).

Salary schedules for staff within Starr Commonwealth are rated as competitive with those in comparable positions across the United States. Staff development occurs on an ongoing basis in a variety of forms from professional seminars to the use of university personnel for training.

Program personnel fill broader roles than specialists in larger schools. Thus, the educateur serves as individual and group counselor and maintains liaison with the family and community agencies. The teacher is involved in a variety of activities beyond traditional instruction, and, in reailty, the roles of the teacher and educateur often overlap.

The physical plant includes academic classrooms; a gymnasium; an athletic field; a track; tennis courts; an Olympic-sized pool; and resources for arts, crafts, music, and drama. Extensive use is made of community resources, and students are involved in outdoor education activities culminating in a one-week spring camping trip to the Smokey Mountains.

AEP utilizes the help and cooperation of other agencies. The Area Vocational School acts as a resource for the students who wish to take advantage of this vocational program. The liaison for interagency coordination is structured by AEP staff, who establish linkages and contacts with parents, key community leaders, and involved school personnel. The unique supportive relationship of the Van Wert County Juvenile Court is marked by daily contact.

STUDENT MANAGEMENT

Youth in the alternative program are involved in a teaching-treatment process designed to create a positive student culture. As such, this is a *socioeducational* strategy with the following major goals:

1. Positive teacher-student relationships.
2. Positive peer group relationships.
3. Positive relationships with parents and community.
4. Positive academic achievement and attitudes.

Unlike some peer group treatment programs that tend to de-emphasize the adult-youth interactions, the staff in AEP see their relationships with students as pivotal in creating a positive interpersonal climate.

Although students frequently enter the program with the attitude "I hate teachers," they soon discover a level of intimacy and involvement that is neither typical nor perhaps allowed in public schools. Through field trips, parent contacts, and close interpersonal relationships, staff are able to communicate a commitment beyond the call of duty. Staff must model a genuine concern if the peer group process is to become genuinely helpful. Likewise, staff are always available for individual counseling beyond the group counseling sessions.

The success of the program is dependent upon building a climate of trust rather than confrontation. In a homogeneous population of troubled youth without the balance of conventional students, there exists the clear risk of creating a negative peer culture. Unless the alternative school is strongly positive and productive, the result will be a destructive environment with all the problems inherent in segregating, tracking, and labeling deviant youth.

Students in AEP are involved in a peer group treatment process designed to emphasize positive values of caring, helping, and responsibility. Formal group sessions are held for 1 hour daily, with the educateur serving as group leader. The goal is to develop positive peer leadership skills in problem identification and resolution. The structure of group meetings includes identifying specific goals for change, focusing help on a particular student, and feedback by the adult leader (Vorrath & Brendtro, 1974). The student and his or her fellow group members are enlisted as active treatment agents. As such, they become involved in assessment procedures, definition of tasks, implementation of treatment methods, evaluation of task completion, and even in preparing a student for return to the community school.

The helping process is extended beyond the group meeting as youths assist one another in a variety of ways, including support for positive behavior, peer tutorials, and informal relationships in the community. The intent is to create a climate of shared concern where youths provide one another with positive peer reinforcement of prosocial behavior. As young persons learn to be of value to others, they increase their own feelings of worthiness and positive self-concept.

Through regular service learning projects, the helping process is generalized to other citizens in the community at large and helping expands beyond the group. Students and their staff engage in a wide variety of volunteer activities, typically with senior citizens and smaller children. Thus a group may help an aged couple by chopping firewood or painting their home, or provide recreation for disadvantaged children in a Head Start program. These projects cannot be contrived, artificial, or make-believe work, but must be a genuine response to meeting human needs. The thrust of the group program is to involve youths to a greater degree in creating change than in being changed. In reaching out to another person, the youths create their own proof of worthiness—being of value to someone else. Rather than hoping troubled young people will come forth with a cry for help, youths are asked instead to help one another.

Parents are viewed as full partners in supporting the students and program, in contrast to traditional approaches that frequently focus on treatment of families. While counseling is available for families, emphasis is concentrated more on involvement with parents and siblings rather than treatment. It has been the experience of AEP staff that the student's family has frequently disclosed the key to some of the most difficult problems. After overcoming initial hesitancy, it is not unusual for parents to regularly visit the school and make frequent telephone contact.

The active enlistment of family involvement has proved to be a rich resource for creative methods for helping students. Families participate in a variety of activities, from special recreation days using the campus facilities to participation in serious discussions regarding specific problems related to the student or his or her peer group.

The educational program consists of diagnostic-prescriptive teaching. Students enter AEP with a long history of behavioral and adjustment difficulties. Very often their societal conflicts are school-related, such as truancy, learning impairments, underachievement, or some combination of these and other elements that have resulted in an inability to cope with the demands of the educational mainstream. Consequently, academic deficiencies are generally consistent with the youth's maladaptive behavior patterns. A youth may view school as a humiliating and frustrating place, as academic deficiencies have resulted in intense distrust of school personnel and active avoidance of classroom participation. In response to this vicious cycle of inadequacy and failure in school, all educational operations are based upon a diagnostic-prescriptive teaching model in which the academic needs of each student are carefully analyzed and served on an individualized basis. In pursuit of academic success, an educational plan is devised that incorporates all aspects of the student's academic performance from preplacement through graduation.

Before a student is accepted into the program, attempts are made to secure all available school data. These generally take the form of report cards, teacher evaluations, cumulative records, diagnostic or achievement tests results, and agency reports concerning the youth's academic history.

Again, parents, court personnel, and previous teachers are asked to participate in the development of the individual educational plans for each student. Evaluation of the educational program involves determining the extent to which an individual student has overcome his or her academic deficiencies at the time of graduation. Success means that a student not only has achieved the goal of remediating specific academic weaknesses but also has changed the negative concept of school as well.

PROGRAM EVALUATION

Initial evaluation has targeted on areas of attendance, achievement, and attitudes. Preliminary information is now available on eight students who have been enrolled in the program an average of 7½ months. Attendance records were obtained from the students' previous high schools for the academic year prior to entry into AEP. The average youth had been reported absent 25.4% of the days school was in session. In contrast, during their time in AEP, students were in attendance 94% of the days with absenteeism at 6%.

Upon entry the average youth was in the 11th grade, with reading and math achievement over 4 years below grade level. Reading achievement increased from a grade level of 6.6 at admission to 8.0 at the end of the academic year as measured by the Woodcock Reading Mastery Test. Since the typical student has only been achieving an average of .6 of a grade level per year in previous schooling, the reading gain of 1.4 grade levels in AEP is more than twice that which might reasonably be expected. In contrast to the marked gains in reading achievement, scores on the Key-Math Diagnostic Arithmetic Test showed minimal gains, from 6.9 at pretest to 7.1 at posttest. This lack of measured improvement in math achievement in a course of studies emphasizing math skills raises obvious questions. One possible explanation is that the content of the test items does not reflect the math curriculum, which is heavily oriented toward practical consumer skills.

Through a questionnaire survey parents were asked to evaluate their experiences with the previous school and AEP as well as the attitudes of their son or daughter toward both settings. Seven of the eight parents were available to complete the questionnaire. Six of the parents, 86%, felt AEP staff understood the problems and needs of their children to a great extent or very great extent, while none expressed this feeling about the regular public school. All of the parents described communication between themselves and AEP staff as excellent or good, while 86% characterized communication with previous school personnel as fair or poor.

When asked about their child's attitude toward AEP, 86% indicated that it was somewhat positive, while attitudes toward regular school were described as somewhat negative or very negative in 71% of the cases. Parents were asked to indicate areas for change in AEP as well as elements of the program they liked best. The majority of the parents mentioned family meetings as among the most positive aspects of the program. Although more rigorous research with large populations of students will be necessary, these preliminary data clearly suggest that the alternative has improved student attendance, achievement, and attitudes.

Student grades are awarded on the same basis as in a regular school program and students receive credit for graduation based upon the number of academic hours completed.

PROGRAM FUNDING

AEP combines special education resources with outside community support. The noneducational services have been underwritten by corporate donations, with the administrative overhead donated by Starr Commonwealth's residential treatment program. On an annual basis, the per pupil cost including summer counseling services approximates $4,000. Citizens, the business and industrial community, the Juvenile Court, local schools, and The Starr Commonwealth Schools have combined resources to support the program through a community alliance.

The program success has been due to the collaborative effort between the Van Wert County Schools, the Juvenile Court, and The

Starr Commonwealth Schools. Community support has also contributed in terms of political backing and in budgetary matters. One of the significant obstacles in developing the program was the establishment of the communication channels between the three agencies involved. While this was not an insurmountable problem, the process of three agencies collectively developing a program presented communication obstacles.

Although issues of program funding have been resolved for the present, the greatest uncertainty facing AEP at this time continues to be the issue of responsibility for long-range funding.

REFERENCES

Brendtro, L. K. Bridging teaching and treatment. *Journal of Teacher Education,* 1980, *31* (5).

Heward, W. L., & Orlansky, M. D. *Exceptional children.* Columbus: Charles Merrill, 1980.

Vorrath, H. H., & Brendtro, L. K. *Positive peer culture.* Chicago: Aldine, 1974.

Delta County Education Center

408 North 9th Street
Gladstone MI 49837
(906) 428-3146

Ursula Y. Busch, Director

The Delta County Education Center was established in 1978. It is located in a remodeled storefront in a rural community and serves students from five school districts in Delta County. Although the school operates under the umbrella of the Delta-Schoolcraft Intermediate School District, it is guided by a private, nonprofit, corporate advisory board of directors. This advisory board sets policies, develops guidelines, determines budget, and works with the director of the Center to confirm program philosophy, curriculum effectiveness, and staff selection.

The advisory board is comprised of representatives from the Department of Social Services, Delta County Probate Court, Community Action Agency, Delta County Sheriff's Department, local education agencies, parents, and a member of the clergy. This representation is mandatory in order that agencies affected by and involved with the Center's target population may be effectively served.

The alternative school operates out of a remodeled store front. It is a warm, open one-room facility with portable room dividers separating learning areas. There are approximately 3,000 square feet of usable space with an additional 2,000 square feet available for expansion when funding becomes available. To date, that space has been designated to include two enclosed classrooms, one additional bathroom with shower, and a large space for community meetings and library work.

Students live at home and are bused to and from the Center via the satellite vocational education transportation program. The Center is open from 8:00 a.m. until 4:00 p.m. Classes are held between 10:00 a.m. and 2:30 p.m. The program operates during the traditional school calendar of August through May (9 months). Our present class schedule includes three classes on Monday, Wednesday, and Friday and two classes on Tuesday and Thursday. It is designed after a typical college schedule to allow for large time blocks in each class.

TARGET POPULATION

The Delta County Education Center is a voluntary program that serves no more than 50 students at any given time during the school year. A waiting list is maintained for interested applicants. Students are between 16 and 18 years of age. They are primarily Caucasian, with a small percentage of Native Americans. Students who enroll in the Center do so after electing to leave the traditional program. Many bring a history of truancy and lack of school success due to their disillusionment with the public school system. The alternative school offers a nongraded, individualized way in which these young people, who are of average and above average intelligence, can achieve a high school diploma. Approximately 50% of the students have been involved with the courts.

CLASS PLACEMENT

Students remain in the program for the length of time necessary to achieve required credits for high school graduation. No student is denied the right to apply. If a student is living independently, no parental signature is needed. Students not officially dropped from the local education agency enrollment lists are required to have parental and local education agency authorization to transfer into the alternative school. Students may return to the regular school program at any time within the parameters of that school's enrollment policy.

Screening and Referral Policy

Because each student has individual needs, there may be times when the Delta County Education Center will consider exceptions to this referral and screening policy. Exceptions to this policy will be made using the following procedure:

1. The student will make his or her application *through* a referral source.
2. After the application has been made, a meeting will be held with the individual making the referral. Consensus of the Delta County

Education Center staff must be reached before the procedure can continue.

3. Once consensus has been reached, a written recommendation from the referral source will be placed on file, and the student will complete necessary paper work.
4. Completion of the procedure will require the Delta County Education Center director's approval.

Once the referral process has been completed, applications will be reviewed by the director and the following screening process will take place:

1. The director will screen applications based on referral criteria.
2. Students will be interviewed by the director and at least one additional staff member.
3. Based on their applications and interviews, students will be: (a) enrolled into the Center, (b) referred to cooperating agencies for supportive services, or (c) referred back to local educational programs to work with respective counselors or administrators, if they are in good standing with their schools.

Students will be enrolled into the program based on criteria listed and documented with necessary records. The director will consult with prospective participants and their parents or guardians to determine appropriateness of referral. A student may enroll only after all parties (i.e., student, parents or guardians, and director or counselor) agree that they have established a thoroughly mutual commitment. After enrollment and within 30 days, the student will, under the direction of a professional staff member, complete a standardized diagnostic pretest, identify specific needs and goals, and develop an appropriate schedule.

PROGRAM RESOURCES

The Delta County Education Center employs a full-time director and secretary, three full-time instructors, and one half-time instructor. The director also teaches part-time. Additional staff members include sophomore Human Services interns from Bay de Noc Community College, senior Social Work interns from Northern Michigan University, volunteers from the Gladstone Senior Citizens Center's R.S.V.P. program, and counselors and case workers from the Department of Social Services and Probate Court. Our advisory board of directors acts as a comprehensive liaison between the Center and agencies and schools in the community with whom we work. Parents are contacted frequently via telephone visits and are met with quarterly for a comprehensive review of school progress.

Teachers are selected on the basis of certification within academic disciplines, ability to work with a wide variety of people, counseling skills, and commitment to providing alternatives within an accepting environment. Student-teacher ratio is 15 to 1. All instructors are enrolled in master's degree programs in education—50% of them in the Alternative Schools Teachers Education Program (ASTEP) with Indiana University, Bloomington. Their orientation, commitment, and experience are in alternative education.

At least one staff member each year is one of Indiana University's ASTEP interns. These individuals (certified instructors) work at the Center for 1 year to complete partial requirements for the Master of Arts degree. ASTEP interns make one-half salary due to their internship status, but are in no way less than full-time staff members. They reflect the quality and commitment of people involved in alternative schools throughout the country. All other staff members receive pay comparable to that of regular classroom teachers. Their salaries are determined by the contract established for all teachers working for the Delta-Schoolcraft Intermediate School District.

Inservice teacher education occurs when need, opportunity, and finances become available. Inservice sessions have included topics such as curriculum development, voluntary staff evaluation, substance abuse, confrontation, testing, and alternative education.

A unique and critical component of the Delta County Education Center is our participation in the ASTEP program from Indiana University. This participation not only provides an opportunity to hire excellent instructors, but also allows our program to be part of a national network of high quality alternative high schools throughout the United States. ASTEP staff members make themselves available for inservice training, consultations, and research projects.

PROGRAM CONTENT

Philosophically, the Delta County Education Center believes that we are all individuals with different learning styles and that to develop our potential we must learn to grow in harmony with our environment and those people with whom we live.

Structurally, we believe in democracy. By dealing with individuals and collective bodies of people in a democratic way, we learn ways in which to satisfy personal needs as well as the needs of the community.

In order to help us to achieve those broad goals, the Center has an articulated curriculum with each of the five school districts it serves. Students must achieve the amount of credit required by their home schools, since the home schools now issue their diplomas.

The direction of the Delta County Education Center curriculum has both stabilized and taken on new dimensions since its inception. The original curriculum, which included the essential skills areas (Michigan Minimal Performance Objectives), Michigan Life Role Competencies, CORE, and Productive Thinking Skills, is still the foundation for academic development and values clarification. It is divided into the four disciplines shown in Figure 1.

FIGURE 1
Delta County Education Center Curriculum

1. Language Arts through:
   A. Basic Skills
   B. Creative Writing*
   C. Language and Literature*
   D. English I
   E. English II
   F. Communications**

2. Social Studies through:
   A. Social Studies I
   B. Social Studies II
   C. Geography**
   D. Government
   E. Sociology**

3. Mathematics and Science through:
   A. Everyday Mathematics
   B. Basic Mathematics
   C. Algebra**
   D. Physical Science
   E. Ecology
   F. Biology

4. Electives through:
   A. G.E.D.
   B. Careers
   C. Psychology
   D. Leisure Arts
   E. School Public Relations

*Creative Writing and Language and Literature were added to the Basic Skills component for those students in transition from Basic Skills to English I.
**These classes were offered for either advanced credit in a special discipline or elective credit.

In addition, there are several unique components that allow individual flexibility:

G.E.D.

Several students, after enrolling and attending regularly, decided that the number of requirements necessary for them to achieve the conventional high school diploma would take a considerable length of time. Since they were approaching 18 years of age, an investigation of the G.E.D. program was made. After careful consideration, they were allowed to prepare for the G.E.D. program. However, the following specific conditions were established prior to their enrolling for this class:

1. One semester of classes, passed satisfactorily, must be completed.
2. G.E.D. examinations cannot be taken before the student reaches 18 years of age.
3. Students must reach minimum competency levels in mathematics and English before enrolling in the G.E.D. preparation class.
4. The G.E.D. preparation class can be taken only as part of a complete semester's work.
5. Students must assume responsibility for the cost of the G.E.D. examinations.

CORE

A weekly session designed to promote student-staff *C*ommunication, *O*rganization, *R*esponsibility, and *E*valuation. The CORE group affords students the opportunity to discuss thoughts, feelings, and goals individually and in a small group. Emphasis is placed on self-image, relationships with others, and values clarification. Counseling is an ongoing activity during CORE group, while students are able to work on individual projects or deal with concerns facing the entire school community.

In addition to its original goals, two developments in the concept have further illustrated the importance of the relationship between the CORE leader and his or her CORE group members:

1. Those students who were with the same CORE leader over a prolonged period of time (1 to 2 years) demonstrated observable changes in attitude and academics.
2. Student staffing, a procedure designed by Carol L. Malnor during the 1978–1979 school year, is implemented by CORE leaders. This component provides documentation of a student's progress and adds clarity and direction to the value of CORE. All results of staffings are placed on file at the Center after being shared with individual students. One staffing is completed on each student during the year.

Independent Study

Independent Study is a component specifically designed to allow interested students the opportunity for research into subjects that create interest and motivation for them and that may be unavailable in regular classes.

Independent study may take a variety of forms such as research papers, a visual project, or community work, but it *must* include the following elements:

1. It must be student initiated. The *student* must approach the teacher if he or she is interested in working on an independent study.
2. A contract must be completed, agreed upon, and signed by both the student and the instructor.
3. In order for credit to be granted, the contract must be completed satisfactorily, based on an evaluation by both the student and the instructor.

Student Self-Scheduling

This component allows students an opportunity to choose their own classes from the established schedule. Credits are reviewed with their CORE leaders and, based on proximity of graduation, scheduling is completed. Student input is encouraged and accepted.

School Government

Although the Center has operated democratically since its inception, its evolution into a fully realized process for students has only recently occurred. Students are now beginning to understand the significance of having a voice in the establishment of policies that affect them individually and collectively. Manifestations of this are visible in:

1. The student government committee. This group is comprised of government officers and works directly with staff toward the resolution of major concerns of the Center.
2. The student judicial board. This group reviews and tries school policy infractions.
3. The revised review procedure. This includes a government interview for all new applicants, an automatic probationary condition of 9 weeks for new students, and the same for returning students who fail to pass four out of five of their classes during a semester.
4. The student interview team for new staff applicants. The students have prepared and implemented an interview process for each new staff applicant from Indiana University's ASTEP program.
5. General committees. These committees are comprised of volunteers who express a concern and demonstrate a desire to work toward the achievement of specific goals such as building improvement, curriculum, or extracurricular activities. (*Note:* Examples of the efforts of these committees include painting the exterior of the school and formulating a new class schedule.)

The success of the democratic process is now becoming visible. It is the Center's wish to continue working toward greater awareness and development of skills necessary to continue this vital component.

Curriculum is the mainstay of any school system. It must continually work toward the achievement of its stated purposes through evaluation and refinement. To assist us in continuing the development of a quality educational environment, application has been made for membership with the North Central Association for Accreditation of Optional and Special Function Schools.

Instructional methods that have been found to be most effective are as unique as individual teachers and students. Some common characteristics of effective approaches, however, include informal atmosphere; providing a variety of options for achieving class requirements; openness to questions, frustrations, and concerns from students; equal exchange between teachers and students; minimal "lecturing"; providing materials that are relevant to students' lives; providing clear expectations and rationale for lessons; and above all, trust!

STUDENT MANAGEMENT

Behavior management techniques include the Attachment Group, as shown in Figure 2; Self-Evaluation Tool, shown in Figure 3; a Judicial Board; and Contracts.

FIGURE 2
The Attachment Group

1. Goals: *Communication of behavioral expectations.*
   O rganization of class time.
   R esponsibility for behavior and class work.
   E valuation of behavior and class work.
2. Strategy: Students who have not been responsible for their own behavior at the Center will be attached to one or two adults who will monitor their behavior until such time that these students show marked changes and/or responsibility.
3. Tools: (a) Self-evaluation instrument by Chandler.
   (b) Weekly feedback sheets from each instructor on behavior and academics.
4. Evaluation: Weekly feedback sheet.
Success will be achieved when students have completed four consecutive weeks of classes with favorable feedback granted from each instructor via the feedback sheet. Feedback must be granted by *all* instructors; not just one or two.
NOTE: Participants may not be absent from this group for any reason. Absence from the group will be understood as a voluntary termination of their program at the Center.

FIGURE 3
Self-Evaluation Tool for Attachment Group

Give yourself an age for each of the following areas of development. (How old would you rate yourself?)
1. Chronological age in years:_____
2. Physical age (How old do you look?)_____
3. Mental age (How old do you think? How well educated are you? How old do you sound?):_____
4. Social age (Do you meet your responsibilities at home? At school? At work?):_____
5. Emotional age (temper, procrastination, cursing, getting high so things are easier, etc.):_____

Add up each score and divide by five. What are the results?

Judicial Board

The Judicial Board is comprised of elected officers who meet to hear attendance infractions of more than four unexcused absences. The board hears the cases (as presented by individual students) and determines appropriate consequences. Consultations with CORE group leaders may be requested to assist the board in making their decisions.

Contracts

Contracts are established based on need as seen by teachers and students to help enhance the experience for success in the Center (see Figure 4). They are entered into voluntarily by students with the approval of their parents, instructors, and the director.

The underlying theme of these techniques is referred to as "Structured Freedom." Originally designed by Phil Schlemmer, director of the Zoo School, a program for highly motivated sixth graders, it suggests that as a student assumes more responsibility, he or she is provided an opportunity for more freedom in the decisions made in his or her educational career in the Center.

Crisis Support

Crisis support for all students is offered through the local family services center, substance abuse and medical programs, Department of Social Services, and Probate Court. This help is given voluntarily and generously to students expressing a need and/or interest.

93

FIGURE 4
Sample Contract

DELTA COUNTY EDUCATION CENTER
408 North 9th Street
Gladstone, Michigan
49837

CONTRACT BETWEEN: DELTA COUNTY EDUCATION
         CENTER AND

_____

REASON FOR CONTRACT:
 The purpose of this contract is to redefine the expectations of the
 Delta County Education Center. In order for the above named
 student to continue with the alternative school, the following
 conditions must be met.

CONDITIONS OF CONTRACT:
 1. ATTITUDE: _____

 _____

 2. ACADEMICS: _____

 _____

 3. ATTENDANCE: _____

 _____

CONSEQUENCES OF CONTRACT:
 In order to remain in the Delta County Education Center, the
 above conditions must be met. Failure to meet these conditions
 will result in the termination of the school program.

_____ _____
 Director's Signature   Student's Signature

_____ _____
 CORE Leader's Signature Parent's Signature

APPEAL:
Students have the right to appeal this contract if it is broken and they
feel that their withdrawal from school is unreasonable.

PROGRAM EVALUATION

Students are evaluated in academics, attendance, and attitude. Quarterly progress reports are completed by both students and staff and grades of A, B, C, or No Credit are issued. Incompletes are given if a student feels the work can be made up within a specified period of time. The Center itself grants credit. This credit is accepted by local education agencies if a student chooses to return to the home school campus to complete his or her program.

A year-end report is completed annually with statistics of achievement. (See excerpts from latest report in Figure 5.) Factors that have contributed significantly to this progress include:

- Community involvement and support.
- Participation in Indiana University's Alternative Schools Teacher Education Program (ASTEP).
- Highly qualified, motivated, and dedicated staff.
- Continuous evaluation.
- Student involvement.
- Shared decision-making (democratic system of operation).

The major pitfall has been money. Although we would not do things differently, achieving financial stability through continued long-range planning will be a key in achieving permanence as a true alternative in the community.

PROGRAM FUNDING

The Delta County Education Center was established through funding within the Neighborhood Education Authority in the Michigan Department of Education, Lansing. That funding later continued through Secondary School Options (MDE) but was recently eliminated due to budget reductions in the State of Michigan. Presently, the program is operating at a deficit for that reason. Additional sources are being investigated and requested through private foundations, Michigan Department of Education grants, and local agencies. Funds flowing into the alternative school include:

1. Section 48: Juvenile Rehabilitation (Michigan Department of Education).
2. Alternative Education for Pregnant Adolescents (Michigan Department of Education).
3. Adult Basic Education (Michigan Department of Education).
4. Ninety-five percent of State Aid portion of total per pupil allotment from local education agencies.
5. Child Care Funds (Delta County Probate Court).
6. Memorial Fund (local patronage).

Billing is provided through the Delta-Schoolcraft Intermediate School District's business office directly to funding sources. The average per pupil cost is approximately $2,000.

FIGURE 5
Fact Sheet

DELTA COUNTY EDUCATION CENTER
1979–80 FACT SHEET

1. The students at the Center maintained 72.5% attendance (up 2.5% from the 1978–79 school year).

2. The 63 students at the Center achieved 862 grades, as follows:

> 27.2% of the grades were A's
> 32.6% of the grades were B's
> 34.2% of the grades were C's
> 5.2% of the grades were No Credit's
> .8% of the grades were Incomplete's

NOTE that 94% of our students achieved a C or better in their classes. All students achieving a grade of A, B, or C received a full quarter (.25) credit for each of the passing grades achieved.

3. Three summer positions with Mead Paper Corporation were granted to 1979–80 Delta County Education Center graduates in support of the outstanding work achieved by those students.

4. Tim Mineau, School President, tied for *Outstanding Student Machinist* in his vocational education class. (The class is offered through the Delta-Schoolcraft Intermediate School District's Vocational Education Program.)

5. Of all students who have graduated from the alternative school, 50% are enrolled in programs through either Northern Michigan University, Bay de Noc Community College, or the Armed Services. Areas of concentration include special education, medical corps, aircraft engine maintenance, forestry, diesel mechanics, law enforcement, and cosmetology.

6. The Center's staff addressed 70.5% of all Michigan Minimal Performance Objectives during the 1979–80 school year. (Performance objectives covered were in the areas of Social Studies/Government, Mathematics, Science and Communications Skills/Language Arts.)

7. The Center's staff addressed 100% of the original Michigan Life Role Competencies again during the 1979–80 school year. (The MLRC are Aesthetic-Humanistic Appreciations, Civic and Social Responsibilities, Employability and Occupational Skills, and Personal and Family Management.

Chana High School

3775 Richardson Drive
Auburn CA 95603
(916) 885-8401

Hal Flood, Principal

The Chana High School program began in 1967 as a continuation high school. In 1975, it was designated an alternative/continuation high school for grades 9, 10, 11, and 12. In 1979 an independent study program option was added for students with jobs, families, or special needs that make daily attendance difficult. As of January, 1981, an independent study learning center was established as a separate facility on campus.

Chana High School is a part of the Placer Union High School District, which is funded by the state based on average daily attendance. It is accredited by the Western Association of Schools and Colleges Accrediting Commission for Secondary Schools. The school district is rural in nature, with three comprehensive high schools—one in Colfax with approximately 750 students, one in Auburn with 1,650 students, and one in Loomis with 1,300 students. There is one special education residential facility in Meadow Vista that can handle approximately 50 students. A new single-class facility for severely emotionally handicapped students is associated with the Sierra View Mental Facility. Chana High School is open to any of the students within the district. About 12 elementary school districts send students to this district. The high school district serves an area of approximately 930 square miles. It is about 50 miles long and 30 miles at its widest point.

TARGET POPULATION

Chana operates from the first of August through the first week of June. The initial number of enrollees is generally about 100 returning students, plus approximately 50 students from the comprehensive schools for remediation. Enrollment starts low in August, builds to about 300 in January and February, and then levels out to about 200 in June.

About 20% of the students enrolled are under 16 years of age. The remainder are 16 to 19, with a few over 20. There is almost an equal number of males and females. Almost all students are White; the majority are Protestant. Within the area, the largest minority is Japanese, and second, Native American Indians. Very few Blacks or Hispanics attend Chana High School.

Students come from a dozen different elementary school districts, ranging from a one-room schoolhouse to the largest elementary district of approximately 2,000 students. There is very little coordination, if any, between districts.

Of the Chana student population, 80% are low achievers. Attendance in prior schools has been poor, earned credit is lacking, basic skills are poor, and the students often have reading level problems. The reasons for referral of these students are poor attendance and low achievement. The remaining 20% have substantial ability but also are not achieving. Probably 90% of the referrals are either student-initiated or mutual with school and parent because of poor attendance and grades.

Alcohol and drugs combined with poor attendance and poor grades are the greatest problems. Parents and students are told prior to enrollment that Chana will not tolerate disruptive behavior that is intended to hurt others or deny them the opportunity to be involved in classroom activities. On occasion students are removed for short periods of time and placed on home study. Fewer than 5% of the students are involved with probation in any given year.

CLASS PLACEMENT

All students (except known dropouts and students from other continuation or alternative schools) must be referred by the comprehensive high school administration. All students living with parent or guardian must meet with the staff for a parent conference prior to admission. All students upon acceptance attend an orientation class (including information on grading, attendance, etc.) and are tested in reading for placement and programming. Most often admission to Chana occurs because the student is not succeeding at the comprehensive school. Referrals are almost always with parent approval.

Students can graduate from Chana or return to their prior school if credit deficiency is made up and attendance and behavior are satisfactory.

PROGRAM RESOURCES

At present Chana staff includes one full-time and one half-time administrator, one full-time and one half-time counselor, eleven teachers, and two clerical employees. The pupil-teacher ratio is never higher than 22 to 1, usually is lower than 20 to 1 during most of the school year. Teachers have secondary school credentials, generally teaching certification within their subject areas. Counselors have pupil personnel credentials, and administrators have administrative credentials. Salaries are the same as in comprehensive schools for all certified and classified personnel.

Help and cooperation from the community are available when needed. Chana's reputation and image in the community are more positive than negative. There is strong support from our school board. Students (more than 30%) have jobs within the community. The police departments, probation officials, newspaper, and other organizations treat the school fairly. Parent involvement is almost zero.

Chana High School is represented at all levels and on all committees within the district and community: administrative; counseling; educational development (teachers); subject area district curriculum committees; and the School Attendance Review Board (SARB), an intercommunity committee comprised of police, probation officers, health officials, county staff, and so on.

PROGRAM CONTENT

Chana High School's goal is to provide an alternative approach to education that not only meets the needs of students unable and/or unwilling to find success in the comprehensive high school, but also assists students with the development of survival skills that will enable them to cope with the responsibilities of adulthood.

The basic objectives are to:

1. Develop communication and computational skills including reading, spelling, oral and written language, and mathematics commensurate with the individual student's ability.
2. Develop special skills and understanding in vocational and avocational areas that can be used in work and leisure commensurate with individual desires and capabilities.
3. Develop self-awareness, self-understanding, and a feeling of self-

worth by recognizing and accepting the students' individual abilities and limitations and by making optimal use of their capabilities.
4. Develop an eagerness for lifelong learning.
5. Develop the ability to form positive relationships with others through an understanding of the worth, rights, dignity, and uniqueness of all humans.
6. Accept responsibility for individual choices and for the consequences of those choices.

The curriculum differs from the regular school curriculum in reading level. In most cases, materials are geared to lower achievers who have reading problems. The curriculum includes social sciences, English, math, business education, agricultural science, and arts and crafts. Students have input regarding new course offerings and the planning of their own individualized programs.

The most unique feature of Chana High School is the octamester schedule. The school year is divided into seven parts called octamester. Each octamester is 5 weeks long, except for the first one, which is 7 weeks in duration. There is a 1-week school vacation between each octamester. At the end of each octamester, students receive credits and grades based on productive attendance and work accomplished.

The purpose in offering this schedule is threefold:

1. It provides for a great deal of flexibility in student programming. Students can sign up for 35 different classes in 1 school year.
2. Students are more aware of their progress by receiving grade and credit reports at the end of each octamester.
3. The 5-week term provides teachers an opportunity to offer short minicourses of their choice as frequently as they desire.

Students are encouraged to attend regularly during the octamester, work in their classes, earn as much credit as possible, and then relax and take a week off. This week off also improves the morale and efficiency of the teachers.

STUDENT MANAGEMENT

The philosophy of Chana is to concentrate on and reward the positives. Rules are minimized. The staff are more tolerant of deviant behavior and provide opportunity for communication, listening, and nondirective as well as directive counseling. They offer solutions rather than punishment. They do not make threats. The student is removed when appropriate (about 20 students or fewer are suspended per year). Acceptance is stressed; each individual is responsible for his or her own actions and the consequences. Due process is followed. The alternatives provided are never a surprise. Those with severe emotional disturbances receive community help through Sierra View Mental Facility.

Extracurricular activities are not an integral part of the Chana instructional program. This is due mostly to the makeup of the student body and the location of the school. Students attend Chana during the hours that classes are scheduled, and then they leave. The school is located on the outskirts of Auburn; therefore, it is not a hub of after-school activities.

PROGRAM EVALUATION

There are seven student grading periods. Students receive credit at the end of each period. The opportunity for credit is almost unlimited. Students compete against themselves. The graduation diploma is the same as in other schools. Indications of the program's success may be found in the 5-year accreditation, progress reports, comparison of past and present credit accumulation, and attendance records. Students cannot earn credit until they start attending school. Improved attendance is the best indicator of success; personal development and credit accumulation follow. It is difficult to establish credibility with teachers and administrators, who see all the negative aspects of a student. There is a strong tendency to look for weakness in a new school or alternative program. Negative public relations are harmful.

Suggestions for Establishing Credibility

Records are needed on attendance and behavior. Comparisons should be made with the students' credit prior to their admission, and results should be made known. Success should be enjoyed, but shortcomings and failures should be acknowledged. It is important to communicate—seek advice and direction when appropriate and share what is happening. Administrators and counselors should be encouraged to visit while the students are at school. A 10-minute visit is worth more than 1,000 calls and conferences. Staff participating in an alternative school should document, collect statistics, and stand up for and sell the program.

Service and community organizations should be contacted and told about the program, and their comments should be sought. These people—particularly the negative ones—should be invited to visit the school while it is in session. It is crucial to tell the truth and be realistic. Reporting too much success can be a problem, for soon people might think that the alternative program can solve every student's problem or meet every need.

PROGRAM FUNDING

Regular education reimbursement is received from the state. The local school district provides the same allocation per student. However, Chana School receives this amount *times 36%* to provide for smaller classes, increased supplies, and so forth. The average cost is $1,140 per student in the regular program and $1,550 per student at Chana. There is a decentralized budget system for each school and the budget is tied to average daily attendance with a (+) or (−) carryover balance.

Walbridge Academy

Grand Rapids Public Schools
1024 Ionia, N.W.
Grand Rapids MI 49503
(616) 456-4922

Russel Harmelink, Principal

Walbridge is the oldest alternative school in Western Michigan, having been in operation since 1967. It serves 250 students, grades 7 through 12, from the city of Grand Rapids. The Academy was accredited by the North Central Accrediting Association in 1979. Funds for operating the school come from the State of Michigan, local board of education funds, Section 48 (special State of Michigan funds for work with delinquent youth), and Title I funds. The program is housed in an old elementary school building near downtown Grand Rapids.

TARGET POPULATION

Walbridge has 450 students per year with a capacity for 250 being enrolled at any given time. A large turnover of students is common. The average class size is 15. Students are normal range IQ, underachievers in school, and usually from lower socioeconomic level families. Many have had problems (academic and behavioral) in former schools, and many are labeled "potential dropouts." At any given time there are 30 to 40 students enrolled who are also on probation to the local Juvenile Court. Approximately 40% represent various minority populations. The administration prefers a heterogeneous student population as related to delinquency, achievement, and social behavior. It is easier to change students' behavior when appropriate role models are present. Most of the students have come from traditional schools and have not participated in typical extracurricular activities in those schools.

CLASS PLACEMENT

The month of September is open enrollment—first come, first served. Students who have done well the previous year are invited back. From October through April, students enter through the system's Student Services Department. Referrals are made by courts, school counselors, and parents. If students do not perform well at Walbridge (attendance/behavior) they are asked to leave, and other students are given a chance. No handicapped students attend Walbridge.

Students may stay at Walbridge for a maximum of 6 years (grades 7 through 12) and earn their high school diploma. Students may leave at any time. Walbridge Academy is a regular public school. Success is not defined as students returning to their formal school!

PROGRAM RESOURCES

Walbridge employs one principal, two counselors, a part-time nurse, and thirteen full-time teachers and one half-time teacher, most of whom hold master's degrees. A strong teacher's union exists in this school district. Teachers may transfer based on seniority and qualifications in subject matter. Teachers' salaries at the Academy are the same as regular teachers'. A citizen's advisory committee made up of parents, students, and community citizens actively supports the operation of the school.

PROGRAM CONTENT

Walbridge Academy's primary purpose is to help students who have experienced failure or very little success in another educational environment. It attempts to provide its students with successful experiences. Its goals are for students to:

1. Increase basic skill levels in reading and math.
2. Improve attendance patterns.
3. Earn credits toward a high school diploma or promotion to a higher grade.
4. Increase socially desirable behavior such as following rules, dependability, and good work habits.
5. Increase decision-making skills.
6. Improve self-image.

Walbridge is part of the regular school program and differs from other secondary schools in its delivery system. Due to the limitations of the facilities, physical education is not offered. Otherwise, the regular high school subjects are taught.

The individualized, self-paced, success-guaranteed approach to learning is very therapeutic, and helps most students who come to Walbridge. Teachers are allowed and encouraged to deviate from the system-recommended curriculum. Students earn one-tenth of a Carnegie unit after completing 15 units of work. Students must accomplish their work at 70% or better proficiency or repeat the work.

In most classes, the student can earn up to 10 points for every assignment completed. Sometimes a teacher will grant a bonus for completing a credit. Most students use their points to go to the Student Center to take a 10-minute break. Some students will choose to save their points and cash them in on paydays (Fridays). Every two points is worth one cent. Points may also be used for special events such as roller skating, movies, and bowling.

STUDENT MANAGEMENT

Filling up a student's time schedule with successful experiences while in school is a tremendous asset in reducing student acting-out behavior. Techniques used include letters and calls home, attendance lotteries, free passes to the student recreation room, attendance check-off sheets carried to classrooms, honor rolls, and suspending students. If students elect to violate school rules, they are expected to take the appropriate punishment.

A time-out (detention) system is used for students violating school rules. The entire staff is involved. A violator must sit for 20 minutes in our time-out room immediately after being detected violating a school rule. Violations include:

1. Being disrespectful or hassling a student, staff person, or any person in the building.
2. Smoking where it is not permitted.
3. Skipping class.
4. Not having or using a pass properly.

A student may only have four of these time-outs in 15 days; then the parents must return to school with the student.

A student receives a suspension for the following behaviors:

1. Fighting.
2. Assaulting another student or staff person.
3. Physically threatening a staff member or student.

4. Violations of city, state, or federal laws (e.g., drugs, fireworks).
5. Too many time-outs.
6. Use of drugs or selling of drugs.
7. Destroying property.

PROGRAM EVALUATION

Marking periods are every month with the exception of May and June, which are combined as one marking period. A report card is sent home after each marking period and lists the complete credits earned as well as behavior and attendance records.

Regular A-B-C grades are given. Promotion is granted *only* on the basis of credits earned. Credits earned at Walbridge are transferable to any other school. About 50% of the students who come to Walbridge improve their attendance and credit production. In the last 5 years, 76 students received high school diplomas.

There is a continual waiting list of students who want to come to Walbridge. In a time of declining student enrollments, this is a good indicator of success in the community.

PROGRAM FUNDING

Walbridge Academy began with Title I funds in 1967. About 20% of our yearly budget continues to be made up of funding other than that of normal local and state funding. It is less costly to have a child in Walbridge for an academic school year than it is to have a child in a standard secondary school for 1 year in Grand Rapids.

Horizons High School

2823 Clydon Avenue, SW
Wyoming MI 49509
(616) 534-7602

Jerry Hartsock, Director

The program is administered by Wyoming Public Schools, Wyoming, Michigan. Horizons is located in a suburban school district; however, the program serves inner-city and rural areas as well.

Horizons is housed in a building separate from the other high schools. Although the facility was not originally designed as a school, it meets all relevant needs. The program is in session from September to June. There is no summer session. Students are responsible for their own transportation.

TARGET POPULATION

The Horizons Program has an average yearly enrollment of 150 students ranging from 15 to 19 years old attending grades 9 through 12. The largest class serves 20 students, with remedial students receiving extra attention.

The general ability level of the student varies widely. The overall population split according to ability is as follows:

> 10% Gifted
> 10% Learning disabled
> 30% Low achiever
> 10% Emotionally disturbed
> 40% Average ability

Of the total school population, approximately 30% are involved with the juvenile system and are on probation for minor violations. In most cases students come to Horizons with 1 or 2 years of traditional school experience. Often this has been an unsuccessful endeavor, leaving many students school-phobic. Students at Horizons are 90% Caucasian, and come primarily from suburban schools.

CLASS PLACEMENT

Most students come to Horizons of their own volition. However, school officials, the courts, and social agencies also refer young adults to the program.

In order to enroll at Horizons a student must have the permission of his or her base school principal or have been out of school for 1 semester. Prospective students must be between the ages of 16 and 19, but 15-year-olds who have reached 10th grade level are also eligible.

After an application form has been completed, applicants are interviewed by one or more members of the admissions committee. For students over 16, this is an information-sharing session. Individuals under 16 are screened to ensure program compatibility. A letter or phone call from the previous school counselor is also required of applicants younger than 16. In certain cases, an Educational Planning and Placement Committee meeting will be held involving parents, counselors, and any other interested parties.

Students younger than 16 may be admitted upon special request or referral. A meeting with an admissions council will be required. This will consist of the director, the prospective student, the student's guardian, and a prospective counselor for that student. During that meeting the following topics will be discussed:

1. A general overview of the Horizons Program, emphasizing the philosophy of decision-making and student responsibility.
2. Reasons the student feels the Horizons Program would be a better program for him or her.
3. A written letter that the student is required to provide from his or her previous school counselor or representative (e.g., social worker, probation officer) stating why they felt the student would better benefit from the Horizons Program.

Following the meeting, the student, the guardian, the director, and the counselor would evaluate the meeting and their feelings about the student's likelihood of success in the Horizons Program. The director and counselor may decide to admit the student on a 4-week trial period monitoring the student's attendance, success in classes, and attitude toward the Horizons philosophy. If the admission is terminated, the student will be referred back to his or her previous school.

The school totally integrates all students regardless of disability. Basic skills classes are individualized to allow remedial students to avoid segregation.

Once students enroll in Horizons, they are allowed to remain until the completion of their requirements for graduation. However, if a student does not meet minimum performance standards, established by contract, he or she may be referred to a program better able to fit the individual's needs. Students may return to their original school or transfer to another program at any time.

PROGRAM RESOURCES

Horizons employs seven certified teachers, one administrator, one classroom aide, a part-time social worker, one secretary, and one janitor. Two of the staff have special education certification, and two are certified as school counselors. The teacher-student ratio is approximately 1 to 20.

Experience has shown that the most essential attribute for progressive teachers is an abundance of energy and enthusiasm. Generally this type of individual finds the most success at Horizons. Teachers at Horizons receive the same salary as other teachers in the district and participate in the local union.

Horizons works closely with all the local social agencies that serve young adults. A career education person acts as a liaison between the business community and Horizons School.

PROGRAM CONTENT

Philosophically, education at Horizons is directed at the development of the whole person. For that reason, the use of decision-making skills is seen as a crucial aspect of the learning experience. We believe that those skills are best practiced through various levels of involvement.

Since schools are for students, student and parent involvement are sought in all areas of school operation. Those areas in which students can exercise control include curriculum planning, individual guidance, career education, and the governing process of the Horizons community.

Student involvement and decision-making, a key to the growth of positive self-concepts, are supported in an informal atmosphere that is nonthreatening and success-oriented. Horizons strives to maintain

109

that atmosphere by encouraging comfortable and personal student-teacher relations.

The success of Horizons, as a school and a community, depends not only on the relationships between students and teachers but also on the relationships students have with each other. This aspect of Horizons depends almost entirely on student output and initiative. It is in this area that students can measure their own growth as responsible and sensitive people.

Courses at Horizons are designed to provide both basic and advanced academics as well as special enrichment classes. Most classes are set up to be completed within 9 weeks. However, some courses such as history and government meet for 1 full semester.

In order to provide students input into the curriculum, a course brainstorming session is held each 9 weeks. The course suggestions from this session are placed on cards hung on the wall, where students may add possible ideas for class content.

Teachers then sign those class cards which fit into their area of expertise. Students may also recruit teachers to offer a class of particular interest to them. Students then preregister for classes they want. Classes with the most student interest in a curriculum area are then offered. In addition to the classes offered at Horizons, students may also enroll in the Kent Skills Center, adult education classes, and local colleges.

The course schedule is designed to provide flexibility and variety within a simple format. Students spend 3 hours a week in each class, with additional class-related projects held during the specialty sections. Contact, Community Meeting, clubs, and individualized counseling are also scheduled during various time blocks.

STUDENT MANAGEMENT

Students are involved in all aspects of the school, including discipline. All matters of discipline are handled through the Judicial Board. The Judicial Board has the authority to hear cases of students who violate school policy and to make appropriate recommendations to the director. The director has final say in matters of discipline. If a student feels that the Judicial Board has made an unfair decision, he or she may make an appeal to the director and the Governing Board.

Members of the Judicial Board include three staff and four student representatives. The student members are elected at Community Meeting and serve 1-semester terms. The Judicial Board meets weekly. The Judicial Board members are governed in accordance with its by-laws. Severely disturbed individuals are referred to the appropriate agencies for additional support.

PROGRAM EVALUATION

Student progress is determined by the classroom teacher based on attendance, performance on tests and projects, and participation. These data are reported to the counselor via an evaluation sheet each 9 weeks. Students also evaluate themselves.

At the end of each school year students are asked to evaluate the program. The results of the evaluation have been overwhelmingly positive, including a high level of student satisfaction.

The current success rate of students entering the program is about 70%. This is quite remarkable considering that all of these students have had negative school experiences in the past. The credit gained at Horizons counts toward a regular high school diploma, granted through the traditional program.

Horizons has been chosen as a local demonstration site for districts wishing to establish similar programs. In addition, staff have been invited to speak about the success of the program at Michigan State University, Indiana University, the Northern Louisiana Board of Education, and to educational groups.

Major difficulties in the beginning of the program resulted from a lack of adequate funding. Although this has not been completely remedied, adjustments have been made.

PROGRAM FUNDING

Horizons is funded entirely through two sources: state aid to schools and Section 48 funds (a state grant for programs serving probated youth). Students outside the school district are allowed to attend without tuition.

Because of the creative use of materials and the limited size of the Horizons physical plant, the program generally expends approximately $300 to $400 less per child than the traditional program does.

Kansas City Youth Diversion Project

4th Floor, City Hall
Kansas City MO 64106
(816) 274-2681

Felicia Safir, Director
Elresa Clark, Role Development Specialist

In 1977 the Kansas City, Missouri, Department of Urban Affairs was awarded a grant by the Department of Justice, Law Enforcement Assistance Administration, to implement a demonstration program that diverts and provides services to some youths who otherwise would be processed through the Juvenile Court. Kansas City competed with over 200 cities across the country and was selected as one of 10 cities to be funded as the national demonstration project.

The overall project management is the responsibility of the Urban Affairs Department of the city. This includes planning and coordination of project activities, contract negotiation and monitoring, operation of the information and tracking system, and program evaluation. The city has contracted with the Kansas City Police Department for operation of a Youth Services component of the project. The geographic area served borders Jackson County, Missouri.

TARGET POPULATION

An average of 300 to 400 students a year are served. They range in age from 10 to 16. Of these students, 60 to 70% have learning disabilities, are underachieving academically, and read on a third grade level. The typical student is Black, comes from a low to middle socioeconomic level family, and has previously been enrolled in, but not attending, public school.

In order to participate in the Youth Diversion Project (YDP), a youth must meet the following criteria:

1. The youth must not be currently under the supervision of the Juvenile Court.
2. The youth must not have been apprehended for a dangerous offense such as homicide, rape, robbery, or serious aggravated assault.
3. The youth must not be a first offender charged with a minor offense.
4. The youth must not be a status offender.
5. Sufficient probable cause must exist for court action to be taken.
6. First offenders apprehended for burlary, grand larceny, and auto theft can be considered as target youth, and a parent or relative must appear to receive custody of the youth.

If a youth is apprehended while under the jurisdiction of the Juvenile Court, he or she automatically is sent to the Court rather than to YDP, since the purpose of YDP is to divert youth before they have had any contact with the court system.

CLASS PLACEMENT

Youths brought to the Police Youth Services Unit for alleged delinquent offenses will initially be processed as usual, with some being warned and released. Normally, all retained youths are referred to the Juvenile Court. Under the Youth Diversion Program, youths considered more problematic by the Police Department will be referred directly to the Juvenile Court. The remaining youths will represent the target population for this demonstration project. These youths will be assigned by a random procedure to one of four alternative diversion systems:

1. Juvenile Court.
2. Police Youth Services Unit.
3. Roles for Youth.
4. Release with no services.

A computer randomly decides which component a particular youth will be assigned to, either the 30-day Crisis Intervention Program of the Youth Services Unit or the long-term program of Roles for Youth. Youths apprehended for violent crimes such as homicide, rape, robbery, or aggravated assault serious enough to require hospitalization of the victim are not considered for admittance into Youth Diversion and are sent directly to Juvenile Court. If a youth is randomized to the Police Youth Services Unit, the caseworker must contact the youth within 4 hours of his or her apprehension. If a youth is randomized to the Roles for Youth component, the youth is contacted by a service manager within 48 hours.

PROGRAM RESOURCES

The service manager, placed in a neighborhood agency to manage and provide services to youth, is the nucleus of the Roles for Youth component of the Youth Diversion Program. Upon receiving referrals from the intake officer, the service manager is responsible for making the initial home visit to explain the program objectives, solicit participation, diagnose the problems, and make recommendations for treatment. After the parent has given consent for participation, a service plan is developed to serve as a guideline for the service manager to provide ongoing services to include, but not be limited to, education assistance, individual and family counseling, employment placement, and recreational and social activities.

PROGRAM CONTENT

The Kansas City Youth Diversion Project is a demonstration project designed to compare alternative approaches to diverting youth from the juvenile justice system. Operation of the program determines:

1. The relative impact of diversion versus traditional juvenile justice system processing on the social adjustment and delinquent behavior of youths.

2. Whether the target population benefits more from diversion with intensive short-term services, diversion with the more extensive services, or diversion without services.

3. Whether each of these diversion alternatives is more effective with certain types of youths.

Program Components

The Youth Diversion Project is a research project that explores alternative methods for dealing with the problem of juvenile crime. In its attempt to divert the youthful offender away from the juvenile court system, this volunteer program has two components, Roles for Youth, with its service managers located in various community centers, and the Police Youth Services Unit, with its social workers located in police headquarters.

Police Youth Services Unit

The Police Youth Services Unit has developed an intake unit that works on a 24-hour a day basis at the Police Department Youth Unit. It is the responsibility of the intake unit to assign a youth to one of the diversion alternatives, make necessary arrangements for diversion, and identify and make provision for any immediate needs affecting the youth's well-being. The Police Youth Service component includes a social service unit located within the Police Department that provides intensive individual and family counseling services and makes arrangements for referral to other community agencies for longer-term services needed by the youth. The Police Youth Services Unit generally provides assistance to each youth over a 4-week period.

Roles for Youth

The Roles for Youth component seeks to develop viable roles for youth consisting of placement in employment, community service, or self-development activities. Youths assigned to the Roles for Youth component receive a detailed assessment of problems (educational, psychological, health), interests, and capabilities. Accordingly, an individualized service plan for role placement and appropriate supportive services is developed. Role placement is carried out through contracts with neighborhood agencies, which provide services at 10 locations. Each youth is assigned to a service manager associated with one of the following neighborhood centers: Guadalupe Center, Urban Services YMCA, 19th Street Boy's Club, Clymer Center, Della C. Lamb Center, Northeast Owl Center, Minute Circle Friendly House, Linwood YMCA, 43rd St. Boy's Club, Blue Hills Housing Corporation.

STUDENT MANAGEMENT

A variety of services are provided by the community agencies such as tutoring; structured recreational and cultural activities; career awareness programs; emergency assistance; individual, group, family, and/ or drug counseling; day-care facilities; arts and crafts instruction; Big Brothers; Boy Scouts; and the National Youth Program Utilizing Minibikes.

YDP provides the following educational services: educational assessment, assistance in placement in alternative schools, advocacy for high quality and appropriate educational placement, tutoring in basic academic courses, General Education Development (G.E.D.) preparation, and basic survival skills.

In the Roles for Youth component the duration of services varies and is dependent upon many factors such as the individual youth's progress, attitude, and youth's desire to make positive changes in his or her lifestyle. In the Police Youth Services Unit, which utilizes a crisis intervention model, a youth can receive services from a minimum of 30 days to a maximum of 45 days.

A randomly selected portion of the youths are immediately released to their parents without receiving services. The experiences of these youths are used for comparison with those receiving services.

Program design stipulates the necessity of not labeling YDP participants. To that end, it is necessary to involve non-YDP youths in all program activities except subsidized employment. Non-YDP youths receive tutoring, opportunity to participate in recreational and social events, employment placement, assistance in the regular job market, and youth advocacy. They are involved in the Roles for Youth Club and the Youth Involvement Committee. All youths participating in the Police Youth Services Unit and the Roles for Youth volunteer for these programs.

PROGRAM EVALUATION

According to the statistics provided by a computerized information system, 71.1% of YDP youth *have not* recidivated, compared to 28.9% who have.

PROGRAM FUNDING

The Youth Diversion Program is funded by the Law Enforcement Assistance Administration. The Kansas City Youth Diversion Project is administered by the Urban Affairs Department of the city, with a major subcontract to the Kansas City Police Department Youth Services Unit. In addition, contracts have been awarded to local youth-serving agencies to provide counseling, supervision, and supportive services to youths participating in the project. Role placements are supported by a Youth Stipend Fund, which can provide employment stipends. Funds are also available from the Office of Juvenile Justice and Delinquency Programs to provide alternative educational and tutoring services.

LIFE Center

6701 Fortuna Road, NW
Albuquerque NM 87105
(505) 831-6993

Gary Hocevar,
Director of Alternative Programs

The LIFE Center for Alternative Studies is an alternative school program that is classified as a school housed within a larger (1,200 student body) comprehensive traditional high school, West Mesa High. The director is in charge of all alternative programs at the school. Established in summer of 1978, the program is administered by the local educational agency, which is Albuquerque Public Schools, North Area Division, with direct administrative responsibility falling on the director and indirect responsibility falling back on the larger main school administration. The program is geographically located in the open spaces of the West Mesa area of Albuquerque, yet it deals with what could be considered inner-city problems. The population density is over 60,000. The program was the first operationally funded alternative program of its type in the Albuquerque Public School System. Being a pilot project, during its first year it was closely monitored. After it proved successful, the nine other area high schools were allotted positions in order to establish similar programs.

TARGET POPULATIONS

There are 180 serviced positions in the LIFE Center covering students in grades 9 through 12. During the school year, the center works with approximately 250 students, many of whom transfer to other local alternatives or complete work at the main school. The average class size is held to 15, although because of the current waiting list of over 400 students, three classes have 20 to 22 students.

The ethnic, socioeconomic, and gender breakdown is as follows:

82% Hispanic	25% Middle income
65% Low income	55% Male
45% Female	3% Black and Indian
15% Anglo	10% High income

The students are predominantly English-speaking. Most of the Hispanic children use Spanish. Four of the seven staff members speak Spanish, although only one has an Hispanic surname.

Of the students enrolled, 10% have some type of learning disability. About 25% are emotionally handicapped. LIFE Center does inter-referral to the special education department located on the main campus. The students show an extremely wide range of academic abilities: 10% are gifted, 30% are above average, 45% are average to low average, and the remainder are low or borderline. At least 75% are low achievers. Since the lower level of the program is a preventive program, only 25% of the students are returning dropouts. All of the students are potential dropouts, and 50% have some type of behavior problem. Most of the students have received traditional education, although some students were in special education. None of the students has been equitably, adequately, or justly served prior to enrollment in the alternative school. Most of the students' families are hit hard by inflation and live in what could be loosely termed a ghetto-barrio suburban area. Over half of the students have in some way been involved with the juvenile justice system. Of these, 25% are on probation and 10% are returning from some type of detention facility. The remainder have been mildly exposed to the system through contact with Albuquerque Police. Through contact with outside community and state agencies, many of the students are properly placed and serviced for additional support help.

CLASS PLACEMENT

Students are recommended for consideration by themselves, parents, teachers, counselors, psychologists, administrators, or community agencies. Referrals reflect concerns in truancy, inappropriate classroom behavior, suspension, negative dealings with the law, poor grades, lack of motivation, and dropout potential. Standardized test scores do not determine eligibility, but they are looked at in the process.

The referral is a closely monitored, step-by-step process, as follows:

1. The form is filed.
2. The student is prescreened by a school support team.
3. The student is recommended for an interview.
4. The student is scheduled for an interview by a panel.
5. The student is interviewed.
6. Discussion takes place after the interview.
7. The student's cumulative folder is reviewed.
8. A decision is made.
9. If accepted, the student and his or her parents are offered a placement; it must be a free choice.
10. If rejected, the student is referred back to the school support team for other possibilities.

Currently 75% of the students are mainstreamed for at least one-third of the school day. Next year only 20% will be mainstreamed, due to a change of philosophy.

Since most of the students are bilingual and bicultural, heavy emphasis is placed on the community level of cultural awareness. This is done because the traditional school has been derelict in that area.

Any student, regardless of race, creed, ethnic background, or financial ability, may participate. Only students legally registered for grade levels 9 through 12 may participate. Students may stay as long as they, the staff, and their parents feel it is beneficial for them. A student may re-enter the regular school at will or on recommendation. LIFE Center also assists in post-graduate placement.

PROGRAM RESOURCES

Professional support is received from outside community agencies. The local traditional school offers counseling support.

LIFE Center has six certified teachers, using the team core planning and teaching method. The teachers are hired as counselor-teachers. The student-teacher ratio is 15 to 1. One full-time director is assigned to the program. Part-time secretarial and janitorial support are contracted for. Teacher candidates are interviewed at least three times. Traits or assets desired are empathy, humor, flexibility, adaptability, caring, warmth, uniqueness, professionalism, energy, dedication, desire, and training. One teacher is certified in special education. Salary is the same as for regular teachers. Staff development takes place internally and within the district area. The main school's support staff are utilized in all areas except administration.

An extremely open and cooperative relationship exists with most of Albuquerque's outside community and resource agencies. The director of LIFE Center is the liaison to these groups. LIFE Center has the most active parent advisory council in the state of New Mexico. It is *not* a PTA; it is an advisory and in some areas a governing board. The 200 parents meet regularly at monthly sessions. They guide, advise, and direct efforts at the Center. They are politically active and constitute the strongest outside support agency.

PROGRAM CONTENT

Alternative educational programs at LIFE Center are designed to provide small, highly individualized, extremely relaxed, yet controlled environments that offer course work in the following areas:

Careers and Work Study	Reading
U.S. History	English
Civics	Social Studies
LIFE Skills	World Concepts
Language Arts	

Experiential learning and wilderness exposure are emphasized. Extensive counseling is employed. The program allows parents, students, and teachers to jointly decide and plan out each child's curriculum, goals, and objectives. It also allows parents and children optional choices in educational modes. It offers major options and experiences through field trips and through involvement with parents and the larger community.

The entire curriculum is based on the alternative schools philosophy. It is an optional public school program in direct contrast to the local traditional school. The students all are offered individualized education programs in the alternative philosophy. The individualized educational component is self-directed. Parent, child, and staff are involved in it, but the final decision is left to the student on a contractual basis. The students are expected to fulfill the competencies set forth by the State Department of Education, Santa Fe.

Individualized instruction and small group projects coupled with heavy doses of affective education are most successful. Staff utilizes the school-without-walls concept and the community-at-large in the educational process. The alternative school philosophy believes strongly in the *process* of education. Product is not emphasized. Teachers adapt their teaching styles to the students' needs and styles.

The student is in the alternative school for 2 hours minimum, then attends regular integrated classes. A returning dropout may earn makeup course credit provided he or she qualifies. Close contact is maintained with the child's regular teachers. The program operates from 8:00 a.m. until 12:20 p.m., with optional mini-courses in careers/ work study offered in the afternoon. Field trips are held every Friday. The school arranges for use of the school van and city transportation.

STUDENT MANAGEMENT

The Center tries to engage in positive discipline. Behavior modification and attendance award systems are used. Serious concerns are dealt with by teacher-as-counselor, group counseling, peer counseling, and a student review board coupled with a student advisory board.

Every Wednesday is designated as RAP Day. Massive doses of counseling and affective approaches are specifically tied to this day. Students are actively involved in many decisions in the problem areas and have used the petition system to express their concerns. A well-balanced and effective crisis intervention network is closely coordinated with the school nurse and three outside agencies. Each student receives an I.D. card indicating his or her placement in the Center with all of the staff members' phone numbers listed on it. The program is noted for its flexibility.

PROGRAM EVALUATION

All students are given pre- and postinventories that are LIFE Center staff-designed instruments in all of the core areas of the curriculum. Students are monitored on a daily basis and evaluated at the option of the student and teacher on a weekly basis. Mandated evaluations occur every third week.

The teachers determine their own grading policy and procedures, but they are required to follow the general alternative school philosophy on grading established at the beginning of each year.

State-endorsed credit is granted for courses completed. Students fulfill the regular requirements for graduation. Promotion is never denied. However, LIFE Center reserves the right to withhold credit or remove a student who chooses to fail. LIFE Center does not flunk a student. At the end of each year a 9-month study including grade and discipline/attendance results is released.

Detailed documents and self-evaluations exist (including outside local education agency evaluation) of the program's strong and weak areas. The dedication of the staff, the support of the community (parents), and the support from the Indiana University Alternative Schools Program have all aided in the students' successes. LIFE Center has a low—almost nil—dropout rate, and a high daily attendance rate.

Staff are encouraged by the increasingly positive attitude of the students and their effort toward academic progress.

A major pitfall to the overall success of the LIFE Center is the lack of legislative and district support, and its position as a very successful small school within a failing comprehensive traditional school.

If it were to be done over, the only suggested change would be to make it a satellite school away from the parent agency after the first year of successful operation.

PROGRAM FUNDING

The only funding received is operational funding support from the Albuquerque Public School System, appropriated by the New Mexico State legislature on a yearly basis.

Per pupil cost at the main school (West Mesa High) for 1979–1980 was $1,440. Per pupil expenditure at the alternative school (LIFE Center) for 1979–1980 was $1,460. In 1 year alone, the alternative program saved the school district $234,000 in otherwise lost revenue due to the simple fact that the students were kept in school. That feat had not been accomplished previously in the main school's 10-year history.

Alternative Program

State College Area School District
721 N. Atherton Street
State College PA 16801
(814) 237-4357

Richard Lear, Program Director

The program was established in 1974. Administered by the State College Area School District as part of its programmatic offerings, the Alternative Program uses only local funding for its operation. The geographic area served is the 150 square miles that constitute the school district. Largely rural, the district also serves the community of State College, Pennsylvania, with its year-round population of 30,000 and its Pennsylvania State University population of an additional 30,000.

TARGET POPULATION

Students presently enrolled in the program number 150. Their ages range from 13 to 18. The State College area is predominantly White and middle class. Most minority students—and there are very few—are children of Penn State faculty, staff, and graduate students.

The Alternative Program is open to any student in grades 9 through 12 in the district who wishes to enroll and who has parental permission to do so. The students cover the spectrum from borderline special education students to highly gifted, from National Merit scholars to dropouts. The percentage of students involved in the juvenile justice system is approximately the same as the percentage in the conventional school.

CLASS PLACEMENT

An open admissions policy exists. Students are neither screened nor referred. There are no special classes for handicapped, bilingual, or multicultural students, so those who choose to enroll in the Alternative Program are completely integrated.

Students may remain in the Alternative Program until they meet the usual graduation requirements and other minimum responsibilities. Students may take classes and participate in sports and activities at the conventional high school while they are enrolled in the Alternative Program, and may return to the high school at any time. The staff provide the usual high school counseling services, but no specific placement service.

PROGRAM RESOURCES

The staffing consists of one administrator, one counselor, and one secretary. The number of teaching positions varies, depending on enrollment. Currently staffed at a 17 to 1 student-teacher ratio, there are 8.7 staff positions, used as follows: 7.5 in teaching areas, 1 community resources coordinator, and 1 part-time clerical aide.

The professional staff members are certified in the state of Pennsylvania and are selected by a student-parent-staff committee. Once hired, staff members are placed on the district's salary schedule and are subject to all policies and procedures of the district. Penn State resources are occasionally used as part of the staff development, although no formal arrangement with them has been made.

Likewise, few formal arrangements with other agencies exist, although regular contact occurs with agencies and businesses in the community. Many of the students engage in community service projects or career internships. These resources are considered part of the total program for students. A coordinator of community resources coordinates most of this work. However, individual staff members, who serve as advisors to students, may have regular contact with counseling or other supportive services available to students.

The design of the Alternative Program is based on 13 goals developed when the program was initiated in 1974. While the emphasis on certain goals may vary from year to year at both a program-wide and an individual level, the goals themselves remain unchanged:

1. The Alternative Program will provide and encourage opportunities for students to establish their own goals and to accept individual responsibility for the design and conduct of their own learning program.

2. The Alternative Program will offer a range of courses from which students may elect a program specifically designed to meet their own needs, interests, abilities, and learning styles.
3. The Alternative Program will meet the curriculum regulations established by the Department of Education.
4. The Alternative Program will make certain that students are competent in the survival skills.
5. The Alternative Program will be based in one of the school district buildings but will consider the whole community as a learning laboratory by making use of both public and private facilities.
6. The Alternative Program will employ a differentiated staff and in addition will utilize the talents of members of the whole community on a contract or volunteer basis.
7. The Alternative Program will operate at optimum economic efficiency by meeting the defined educational needs currently not being met through a full use of community resources and district resources and facilities, and by offering a program with broader-based alternatives.
8. The Alternative Program will provide all students with equal opportunities to learn what they need to learn, when they need to learn it, in an environment that is congenial to learning.
9. The Alternative Program will involve students in the determination of school policies, procedures, and governance.
10. The Alternative Program will allow students to meet the state-mandated attendance requirements through a flexible time schedule that can be arranged to meet the educational, recreational, and employment needs and desires of the individual student.
11. The Alternative Program will provide a guidance program using professional counselors, teachers, and members of the community to help students with their educational programs, personal goals, and personal matters.
12. The Alternative Program will provide for the participation of each student in a three-phase career education module.
13. The Alternative Program will involve every student in some form of community services.

PROGRAM CONTENT

Typically, students earn most of their credits through classes at the Alternative Program. Classes meet two to three times a week, and are frequently discussion or seminar-style classes rather than lecture classes. Students may also learn through classes at the conventional high school or Penn State, by independent contract, by correspondence, or through career internships or community service.

The program operates largely on a traditional school day, though students are free to come and go as they wish so long as they attend classes and meetings and otherwise meet their responsibilities. The one or two evening courses offered are invariably popular with students. Students may use regular school bus transportation, local buses, or their own means of transportation.

STUDENT MANAGEMENT

Other than describing appropriate behavior to students, there is an infrequent need to be concerned with behavior management. When problems arise, the following sequential steps are implemented:

1. The teacher involved talks with the student.
2. The student's advisor talks with the student.
3. The director talks with the student. (This step is often omitted.)
4. A counseling team meeting is held. (A counseling team consists of the student, his or her parents, and the staff advisor.) Additional staff, especially the counselor, participate as needed.

In general, a problem-solving rather than a punitive approach is taken and the student is involved in the development of a resolution to any problem.

The responsibilities listed here are viewed by the Alternative Program as *minimal* responsibilities for all students. Enrollment in the program is considered an explicit agreement on the part of the student to accept these responsibilities. The student is expected to:

1. Come prepared to participate in counseling team meetings. (This means the student will have read the catalog and any other pertinent material and will have some idea of what the student would like to learn and how he or she would like to learn it. It also means that the student has examined some alternative modes of learning—using the community, seminars, independent contracts, or the Free University, for example.)
2. Make and keep counseling appointments.
3. Attend class regularly.
4. Attend clump meetings.
5. Maintain some sort of social responsibility toward maintenance and/or growth of the Alternative Program.
6. Abide by policies and procedures developed for the operation and maintenance of the Alternative Program.

At each counseling team meeting, the team will review the degree to which the student is meeting his or her responsibilities. A student not meeting one or more of these responsibilities will be given one cycle to change his or her behavior so that all responsibilities are met. Except in extenuating circumstances, students not meeting their responsibilities will not be permitted to remain in the program.

PROGRAM EVALUATION

Students have the option of receiving conventional letter grades, pass/fail, or written evaluation, and they earn credit toward graduation as in the conventional school. No formal assessment of the program has been made since the program's third year, although feedback is regularly sought and received from students and parents. Major factors in the program's success have been careful planning, considerable autonomy, strong central office and Board support, a capable and dedicated staff, the involvement and support of parents, and the energy and cooperation of the students.

PROGRAM FUNDING

The State College Area School District received a $15,000 grant from the Pennsylvania Department of Education for a feasibility study. Other than that money, the program is completely locally funded. One of the constraints is that the program has operated at or below the per pupil costs of the other secondary buildings during the past 6 years.

Since the Alternative Program is a public school, there is no additional cost to students. Some options for which credit is granted (Penn State classes, for instance) may carry a charge; if so, this cost is assumed by the student and his or her family.

William Smith
High School

10000 East 13th Avenue
Aurora CO 80010
(303) 341-4611

Rolla R. Rissler, Principal

After considerable study by an Aurora committee consisting of students, parents, community members, and school administrators, it was recommended that an alternative program be developed to serve students who were alienated by conventional high schools and were in danger of dropping out of formal schooling. Originally named Aurora Street Academy, the school opened in 1972 with a staff of three adults and approximately 35 students. In a few years, the enrollment climbed to 100, with a staff of four teachers and three aides. In 1975 the school was renamed William Smith High School, relocated to a larger building, and enrollment extended to 200 students with eight teachers and five aides.

William Smith is an autonomous school of record of the Aurora Public Schools. In 1975 it became one of the first Optional Schools to be accredited by the North Central Association. The school serves students in grades 9 through 12 who have been recommended by any of the three conventional high schools within the district. However, enrollment is open to any student who desires to experience a different type of schooling. Graduation requirements are essentially the same as for other high schools within the district.

The school is housed in a 50-year-old school building (originally Aurora High School), complete with an outdoor activity field, gym, and parking lot. The building contains seven enclosed classrooms, a large open area containing a media center, and two classroom areas. Each of the seven classrooms is a center for a particular subject area discipline (science, art, English, etc.). Smaller rooms are provided for counseling and administration.

Transportation to and from the school site is the responsibility of the students.

TARGET POPULATION

Enrollment is limited to 200 students at any given time. Enrollment is voluntary. As a general rule, students classified as in need of special education are not admitted and are referred to programs designed for that purpose. However, if in the opinion of parents and/or other agencies, the school can successfully provide assistance to such a young person, the student is accepted. Approximately 10% of the students enrolled were formerly classified as in need of special education.

The ethnic ratio is comparable to that found in other Aurora schools, with Asian, Spanish, Black, and White. Approximately 52% are female and 48% male.

All students have completed the eighth grade and have attempted conventional high school programs. The majority of students come from suburban, middle class families and have been identified as potential dropouts or dropouts. Students attending the school have been identified as having one or more of the following characteristics:

1. Inability to function satisfactorily in a conventional classroom.
2. Sufficient potential to benefit from the school's program.
3. Academic skill development below ability.
4. General recognition as an underachiever.
5. Failure to establish goals regarding their educational and occupational future.
6. A pattern of behavior problems.
7. Excessive absenteeism and tardiness in conventional schools.
8. A lack of motivation, direction, and drive.
9. Poor self-esteem.
10. A stressful family situation that appears to have a detrimental effect.
11. A one-parent or no-parent family.
12. Hostility toward adults and authority figures.
13. Some difficulty with the law and community agencies.
14. Lack of involvement in any conventional school activities.

CLASS PLACEMENT

Enrollment in William Smith is open to any student currently enrolled in grades 9 through 12 or any student who was previously enrolled in a high school, provided that he or she is under 21 years of age and resides within the boundaries of school district 28-J. For those who are presently enrolled in an Aurora high school, it is necessary to obtain the recommendation of the building principal. The school is voluntary. However, referrals may be made by parents, courts, psychologists, and other schools. Previous achievement, test scores, and past behaviors are not important items for entrance. What is important is the desire by the applicant to be part of William Smith High School.

Students may remain in the school until graduation if they demonstrate academic progress and abide by the Enrollment Agreement (see Figure 6). Students may transfer to other schools at any time. Credit earned at William Smith is transferable to any other high school.

Students are placed in classes that fit their previous achievements, abilities, and interests. Classes are not segregated by age or class standing. Every effort is made to assist students to make choices among classes which will result in success and permit progress toward meeting graduation requirements. If initial placement is not contributing toward personal progress, the student is counseled into other classes. Evaluation is made by the student and teacher.

All teachers act as counselors. The overall counseling program is under the direction of a fully certified counselor. A special class, Senior Exit, focuses upon the formation and development of immediate future goals and directions in both the world of work and continued education for all graduating seniors.

PROGRAM RESOURCES

The school staff consists of eight certified teachers, one or two graduate interns, five instructional aides, a part-time nurse, a full-time secretary, and a principal. The principal teaches classes and acts as a tutor in areas of special interest, e.g., computer science, advanced math, or science. Through a differentiated staffing arrangement, the adult-student ratio varies between 10 and 15 students per adult.

When vacancies in staff positions occur, selection of the new member is by a committee consisting of students, parents, and staff members. Selection is based upon certification area, interest in young adults, and skills outside of the teaching area (outdoor education, special interest areas, etc.). Special education endorsement is not required. Salary is identical to that for conventional staff members with the same educational background and experience.

The school draws upon the total resources of the school district and the community in both personnel and material categories. A full complement of materials and audiovisual equipment is available on-site. When special equipment is necessary, it is obtained from another school or the district media center. The community as a classroom and

FIGURE 6
William Smith High School
Enrollment Agreement

Name _____ Date _____ Quarter _____

Address _____ Phone Number _____

School attended last _____

Total number of credits earned _____ Classification _____

- -

Conditions of Enrollment

Your enrollment at William Smith is voluntary—you are free to transfer out of the school at any time. After you have been enrolled in the school, you are free to change your schedule, with the teachers' approval, when you feel such a change is to your best interest.

You must demonstrate personal progress to remain at William Smith. Progress is demonstrated by earning points in each subject area you are enrolled in and by your attendance in classes. All new students must earn 15 points in each class by the mid-point of the quarter. You are required to earn 30 points in each class for which you are enrolled *or* not miss more than eight class sessions per class per quarter.

You are expected to exhibit socially acceptable behavior at all times. Vandalism, thievery, or threats to others can result in your dismissal from school. Fighting or any act of violence will result in your being immediately dropped from school.

You are not to be on any other school grounds or within any school building of the Aurora School District unless on legitimate business and with that principal's permission.

The use or possession of drugs of any type in or within a two block radius of the school will not be tolerated by students or staff. If you are with someone who violates this agreement, you are considered equally guilty.

Failure to abide by the above conditions will result in removal from the school enrollment. If you are dropped from the enrollment for violation of the conditions, you may request an audience with an Appeal Board to explain your actions. The results of the Appeal Board will be final. If you are not reinstated as a student, you will not visit or remain on the William Smith grounds or within the building.

I have read, understand, and agree to abide by the Conditions of Enrollment as stated above.

Signature_____   Staff witness._____

- -

SCHEDULE

Period 1 _____   Independent Study: Teacher _____

Period 2 _____   Project Title: _____

Period 3 _____   Independent Study: Teacher _____

Period 4 _____   Project Title: _____

Period 5 _____   Vo-Tech: Teacher _____

Work hours: _____   Class: _____

Location: _____

135

community resources are utilized within each of the courses of study. Experiential and outdoor education are an integral part of the overall school program.

PROGRAM CONTENT

General School Goals

The goals of the William Smith High School program are as follows:

1. To provide an atmosphere conducive to the development of a positive self-concept and a feeling of self-worth.
2. To provide a climate that reduces the feeling of student alienation toward school.
3. To provide a school organization that encourages social responsibility.
4. To provide assistance and encouragement to students who are entering the world of work.
5. To develop a positive interaction between students and adults.
6. To improve basic academic skills in students.
7. To provide a means for students to obtain a high school diploma.
8. To develop an attitude that will encourage learning as a lifelong process.

On the average, 32 different courses of study within the areas of English, science, math, and social studies are offered each 9 weeks. Additionally, one class is offered in coed sports and three classes related to the work-study program are presented. All courses of study are developed by individual staff members in agreement with the needs of the students at that time. In all cases, the individual subject area development follows the same basic pattern: cognitive to process, resulting in some product. The product may be an individual or group outcome; it may be short- or long-term; it may be developed on or off the school grounds. An affective component is always part of each course of study, but is not considered a separate, isolated part of the curriculum.

There is not one instructional method universally employed. Staff members attempt to match their teaching methods to the learning styles of the students. Although no one method has proved outstanding with all students, activity and experiential methods have proved to be far superior to read-about/listen programs.

The student school day is from 8:00 a.m. to 12:30 p.m. for 180 days a year. Students are encouraged to attend the local vocational-technical center (part of the Aurora Public Schools), engage in work experiences, or be involved in individual study projects in the afternoons.

Achievement, hence progress, is measured in terms of points earned. Typical letter grading systems are not used. When 30 points are earned and competency in the course content is demonstrated, one-fourth of a credit is awarded. Once a point is earned in a specific area, it is never lost, regardless of time. It is accumulated with points in the same class until a total of 30 are earned. Thus learning is not confined to a given time, and failure is reduced.

STUDENT MANAGEMENT

The practices of democratic principles, student governance, and shared decision-making are the foundation of the school. All rules and policies pertaining to school operation and governance are derived from the students, parents, and teachers. When problem situations arise, either school or individual, the situations are solved by a joint effort. The following organizational structure illustrates the degree of student decision-making employed in the school:

1. *Family Groups.* Each family group consists of one or more staff members and 20 to 25 students. A basic caring and sharing unit, it is the site of problem-solving and decision-making. The group stays together for the entire tenure in the school until graduation.
2. *New Student Interview Committee.* All students desiring enrollment must interview with a committee of two students and one staff member. The committee may reject the application if they have sufficient reasons.
3. *Appeal Board.* The appeal board consists of three students and two staff members. Each student signs an enrollment agreement each 9 weeks. Any violation of the agreement results in the student's being dropped from enrollment. However, the dropped student has the right to an appeal board for immediate re-entrance. The board is the only avenue of reinstatement and its decision is final.
4. *Parents' Advisory Committee.* Parents and students review the policies, operation, activities, and direction of the school.
5. *Student Senate.* The student senate consists of one representative from each family group. It presents issues to the entire school population when necessary.
6. *Discipline Warning System.* Any student or staff member may issue a discipline warning to any other student or staff member who demonstrates unwholesome behavior. Three warnings necessitate a review board appearance.
7. *Review Board.* The review board consists of all members of the staff. It meets to handle special student problems.

When problems of a very severe nature are detected and cannot be handled by the in-house counselor, outside agencies are recommended.

PROGRAM EVALUATION

Student progress is indicated by the number of class points and extra credit points earned. A point is earned by completing an assignment or activity satisfactorily. This determination is made by the specific teacher. When a student accumulates 30 points (this value is determined by the definition of a Carnegie Unit) and demonstrates competency in the area studied, one-fourth credit is awarded. There is no time limit on the time to accumulate the 30 points. Highly motivated students can earn points as rapidly as their ability permits. Thus, a student can earn as much credit as he or she desires. Likewise, slower students are not discouraged by having a fixed time to complete a given subject or activity. By not using a letter grading system, competition is reduced and is replaced with a cooperative attitude. Credit earned in William Smith is transferable to other high schools.

External evaluations are conducted through parents' questionnaires and conferences with parents and students. Research studies concerning school climate, matching student learning styles with staff teaching styles, and overall effectiveness of the school have been carried out by doctoral candidates from various universities.

The success of the school is due to the nonfailure aspect of the program, student buy-in, and the highly personalized nature of the school.

The major obstacle to the development of the school has been the difficulty new students have in learning how to function in an entirely different school environment. This has been overcome by the formation of the family concept and the adoption of an "unclass," which focuses upon unlearning what conventional practices have dictated. Other factors that have contributed to the school's success are: (a) a well-defined curriculum, (b) commitment to the philosophy and goals by the entire staff, (c) the development of open communication and trust by all associated with the school, and (d) strong support from the Board of Education.

PROGRAM FUNDING

The school is totally funded from local school board monies, using the same per pupil allotment as other high schools. On occasion, Title IV funds have been applied for and granted for special purposes (increased media materials). The work-study program is 50% funded by the state (the same as other high schools in the district). There is no cost to the student—other than paper and pencils—to attend the school. Attendance at special activities for which students must pay some part of the total expenses (raft trips, ski trips, etc.) is optional. The cost to the district for operation of the school is slightly less than that required for the same number of students in a conventional high school. This is due, in part, to the lack of support personnel (security guards, transportation to and from school, etc.) and the nonexistence of a separate extracurricular program.

Partners School

1240 W. Bayaud
Denver CO 80223
(303) 777-7000

Suzanne Thompson, Director

The school was started in 1976 through private monies and the support of the Denver Public School System. In 1978, the school was given a federal grant through ACTION in Washington, DC, to operate a Service-Learning component of the curriculum. Due to federal cuts the ACTION funding was withdrawn in the spring of 1979. At the present time, the school is operating through Partners' private foundation grants and the Denver Public School System. Partners School services are available to any qualified student in the city of Denver, but the population is concentrated primarily in the inner city.

TARGET POPULATION

From September of 1979 through May of 1980, 76 students registered in the Partners School program. The age range is 13 to 16. The average class size was 40 students; this year, because of funding cuts, it has been reduced to 25. The class is 68% Chicano, 2% Indian, and 4% Black, with the remainder being Anglo. The students have been nonattenders, have had severe discipline problems, and approximately 95% have been involved with the juvenile justice system. Most of the families are of the lower socioeconomic level and live in project areas of the city.

CLASS PLACEMENT

The students are most often referred to Partners School through the courts, probation, school counselors, social workers, and psychologists. The parents and students themselves also make referrals to the school. After the school receives the referral and prescreening has been completed, the student and parent come in for an interview with the director of the school and one of the counselors of Partners' One-to-One Program. The students are informed about the requirements for admittance into the school. At this time, the students must identify their needs and problems that have kept them from succeeding in the community and school. They must prove a desire to change and commit to specific steps for changing unacceptable behaviors. If the students appear to be good candidates for the program, they are admitted and placed on a 5-day probationary period. If their attendance, attitude, and participation meet the classroom criteria, they are, after the 5-day period, officially enrolled at Partners.

At the end of each semester, student progress is reviewed for further programming and placement. If the students are thought to be capable, they may go on either to the regular public high school, an alternative high school, a vocational school, or to counseling for employment.

PROGRAM RESOURCES

Partners School has one director and three full-time teachers. The program is also assisted by professional volunteers or students who are working on their master's or doctorate degrees. The teachers have been chosen primarily because of their ability to work with in-trouble youth, because they are excellent role models, and because of their ability to cope in the classroom. Two of the teachers are on the Denver Public School payroll and are certified teachers. The other teacher is employed by Partners, and the director is currently on the Denver Public School payroll.

Partners School is directly linked to Rishel Junior High, its facilities and accreditation. Rishel is a nearby regular Denver public junior high school. Partners uses many community services particularly for aerobics and stress management classes.

There is an opportunity for students to spend 3 to 5 days in an outdoor education program at the Partners Ranch. The ranch is located in the mountains on 650 acres. A curriculum of environmental, academic, and social education is designed to give the student a new experience in learning. This experiential learning is directly related to and integrated into their urban setting upon returning to the city.

Video tapes are used in the classroom to evaluate classroom behavior for social role-plays and teaching methods.

Because Partners School is part of the Denver branch of Partners, Inc., it receives the help and support of the Partners staff. Denver Partners matches adult volunteers and in-trouble youth on a one-to-one basis, and Partners School receives many referrals from the counseling staff of Denver Partners. Each student in the school is also matched with an adult volunteer who acts as both friend and advocate.

For the last 2 years, the school has participated in the community on a voluntary basis in service organizations, day care centers, handicapped centers, and nursing homes. The students work at their placement 2 days a week, and part of their curriculum is designed to meet the needs of their service work. They have adult supervisors at their placements and receive credit for their work.

PROGRAM CONTENT

The setting for the classroom work is a combination of a large area used for group activities and several smaller areas used for individualized study. The school operates 5 days a week from 8:30 a.m. to 12:30 p.m. Partners operates on the same yearly schedule as the Denver Public School System.

The students use the public transportation system to get to and from school every day. They are given the tokens necessary to use the transportation system. The students are also taken by van for lunch at Rishel Junior High School every day.

The major goals of the program at Partners are as follows:
1. Students will display improvement in their cognitive skills.
2. Students will acquire more positive attitudes about themselves and others.
3. Students will exhibit improvement in their adaptive work skills; that is, students will learn to adjust their behavior and perceptions to the commonly accepted standards of the world of work (e.g., punctuality, respect for authority, task completion).
4. Students will exhibit a reduction in the incidence of deviant behavior.
5. Partners School will provide a Senior Partner for each student who desires to have one.

STUDENT MANAGEMENT

Students who are admitted to Partners are helped to determine why they need to be admitted. They have to know why they should change, and identify what their problems are and how they will approach change. Self-responsibility precedes the changes. A contract is drawn up with some short-term objectives. The school offers life skills, stress management, and coping skills to assist the students in their work. Partners teaches family and interpersonal relationships and how to cope assertively.

The student is looked on in a holistic manner so that there is a recognition of the interrelationship of such factors as the effects of stress, drug abuse, sexuality, family disturbances, and nutrition. Techniques in assertiveness training give the students the skill to make changes. Techniques for releasing stress such as relaxation, visualization, and aerobics are integrated into the program. Each student is dealt with in an individual disciplinary way. The students must identify what the problem is and decide on solutions. They set up their own rewards and punishments in making these changes. By establishing their own criterion for staying in the school, they also expel themselves if they do not meet it.

PROGRAM EVALUATION

Classroom performance is evaluated on a point system. The students are given points hourly throughout the day so that they know at all times how they are doing. This gives them immediate feedback as to their success and failure. The points are totaled at the end of each 6 weeks and are used to determine a letter grade that can meet the standards set up by the regular system.

Project CITE
(Crisis Intervention Techniques for Education)

Terrell Intermediate School District
Department of Special Services
212 W. High Street
Terrell TX 75160
(214) 563-7504

Sid Whitlock, Project Director

The hospital program was established in 1973, and Project CITE was established in 1979. The program is administered by Terrell Intermediate School District (ISD). The geographic area served is 13 counties in North Central Texas.

TARGET POPULATION

The number of students served in a calendar year is approximately 200 to 250. Their age range is 6 years to 21 years, and grade level is 1 through 12, with an average class size of five students. Anglo is the ethnic dominance, and the language dominance is English. The primary handicapping condition is serious emotional disturbance, and the secondary handicapping condition (approximately 20%) is learning disabilities. The majority of students have been attending public school in their local community, with the largest population from Dallas County, which is the largest county in the catchment area.

CLASS PLACEMENT

Upon entering Terrell State Hospital the client has been referred by a local agency (i.e., public school, community service, physician, or parents). Clients admitted to the hospital do not automatically attend school. Those unable to attend the school are served "on-ward" by an "on-ward teacher." A hospital treatment team for each client determines extent of involvement in the school program. Treatment team membership consists of therapists (hospital staff) and school personnel (local ISD personnel). Referral to the hospital school is made through the treatment team.

Testing consists of the following general battery for school placement purposes:

WISC-R	Raven Progressive Matrices
WAIS	Peabody Picture Vocabulary Test
WPPSI	Woodcock-Johnson
Bender	Brigance
Draw-a-Person	

Admission into Terrell State Hospital follows general requirements of the Texas Department of Mental Health and Mental Retardation. Admission into the Hospital School follows treatment team recommendations. Integration into the mainstream from Terrell State Hospital and the Terrell ISD community is nominal. Approximately two to four students attend one or two classes in the local high school each year. The courses are generally laboratory classes (i.e., chemistry, biology, physics). A student can remain in the program through age 21 or until released from hospital confinement. The hospital treatment team determines the length or continuation of confinement to Terrell State Hospital.

The program is in session during the regular terms, fall and spirng, and 8 weeks in the summer. Students attend classes from 9:30 a.m. to 3:15 p.m., 5 days each week. Transportation for day students not in residential care is furnished by the local education agency wherein the student resides.

PROGRAM RESOURCES

Personnel

The Project CITE Advisory Center Staff consists of Terrell ISD administrative personnel, a vocational placement coordinator, a project coordinator, a social worker, a teacher, a parent, a diagnostician, a recreational evaluation specialist, a consultative expert, and home school district representative(s).

The Advisory Center Staff is employed through Terrell ISD. Funds used at present to support the project are from Public Law 89–313, Public Law 94–142, and Texas Education Agency foundation funds.

Project CITE is in a developmental stage. Local school district personnel are involved in developing (a) local employers' participation in developing classroom training stations, and (b) a videotaping studio for CCTV classwork, diagnostics, inservice staff development, and family training. Local social and community organizations are also involved in the development of Project CITE.

In conjunction with North Texas State University, Project CITE provides special education graduate students with practicum assignments in the Diagnostic Advisory Center and at the Terrell State Hospital Adolescent School.

Specific objectives for CITE counselors are as follows:

1. To provide group and individual counseling for students and families in short-term crisis intervention and/or long-term change-facilitating situations.
2. To facilitate change in maladaptive behavior.
3. To improve social interactions with parents, peers, siblings, and teachers.
4. To develop a therapeutic relationship with the student and his or her family to facilitate growth and change in the child and the family response.
5. To target secondary severely emotionally disturbed students.
6. To train volunteers who are competent to give support to students, families, and teachers in severely stressful situations.
7. To assist teachers in classroom management techniques.
8. To provide individual family consultation for specific family needs.
9. To provide instruction in basic behavior management principles to parent groups.
10. To facilitate family participation in the development of vocational education programming for each student.
11. To develop model programs for use in group situations with parents that will explore and facilitate resolutions of problems that are inevitable responses for families of handicapped children.
12. To investigate existing instruments for measuring attitudes with regard to the handicapped.
13. To explore vocational training modules.
14. To assist in developing and producing a parent handbook.

PROGRAM CONTENT

The School Program uses the open concept of instruction. The primary thrust of Project CITE focuses on a crisis intervention model. It unites the resources, educational materials, and professional staff of three state agencies—Terrell Independent School District, Terrell State Hospital, and North Texas State University—to formulate, implement, and evaluate project objectives.

Terrell Independent School District initiates a delivery system that facilitates linkage with the multimedia and video delivery systems inherent in the staff development (CCTV) department of Terrell State Hospital and the modularized competency-based teacher education program of North Texas State University's Division of Special Education.

CCTV works in conjunction with the Terrell Independent School District in the direct delivery of multidisciplinary as well as educational services for severely emotionally disturbed children and adolescents. The primary and basic delivery system for CCTV is video. Annually, CCTV contributes 200 tapes and equipment for their use to Terrell Independent School District educational programming endeavors. This cohesive delivery system enhances the endeavors of the school district as well as proving jointly advantageous to the union of agencies in multidisciplinary crisis intervention.

Video is an effective means of illustrating behaviors, provides a consumer product with great versatility, and allows latitude for the behavioral evaluation techniques implicit in the formulation of appropriate techniques for crisis intervention and eventual project product dissemination.

An individualized education program (IEP) is developed for each student by the Multidisciplinary Diagnostic Team. The Terrell ISD Department of Special Services houses a Tandy Center Model II Deluxe II microcomputer system. All diagnostic data are entered and a printout is given on each student as to annual goals and short-term instructional objectives for the IEP development.

STUDENT MANAGEMENT

Management techniques employ strict checksheets whereby the client loses privileges such as breaks for refreshments. Clients acting out at school are returned to the ward for confinement as determined by the treatment team. Clients are a part of their assigned treatment team. Grading is not competitive. Students receive credit earned and, when eligible, graduate in the spring graduation exercises of their local district or with Terrell ISD students if they choose to do so. A summer graduation exercise is conducted at the hospital campus for those students completing graduation requirements.

Major Problems

Project CITE addresses a unique need for the severely emotionally disturbed student. By all accounts the project is answering national concerns for a mental health/mental retardation facility. Receiving appropriate funds to assist in the development of such a project, which focuses on national needs, is very difficult. Both federal and state agencies acknowledge the need, but because of the all-encompassing focus of the project they become reluctant to assist in the funding of such a program.

PROGRAM EVALUATION

Existing instruments for measuring student, parent, teacher, prospective employer, and peer group attitudes regarding handicapped persons and vocational training are explored, and new instruments are developed that statisfy the needs of a community fitting the socioeconomic and demographic description of Terrell. These scales are administered anonymously to enhance veracity. Information gleaned from these instruments is used by counselors to determine the structure and content of parent and student group experiences and in-service training modules for teachers and employers. (Figure 7 is a form used to evaluate the program.)

PROGRAM FUNDING

Clients residing at Terrell State Hospital are not required to be on "residential contract" from their local education agency. Hospital residential placement cost is based on a sliding scale.

FIGURE 7
Project CITE Evaluation Form

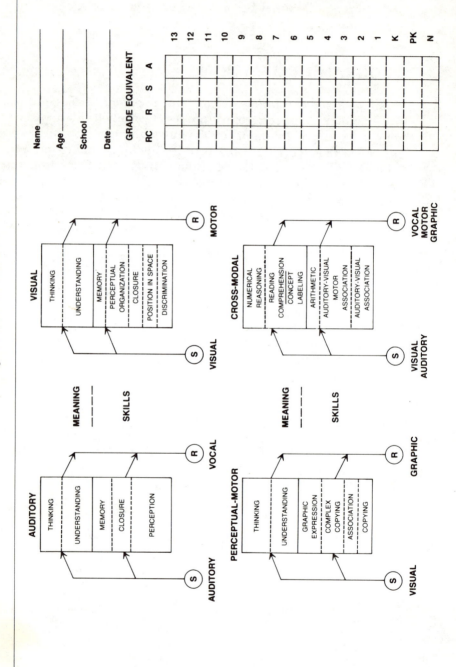

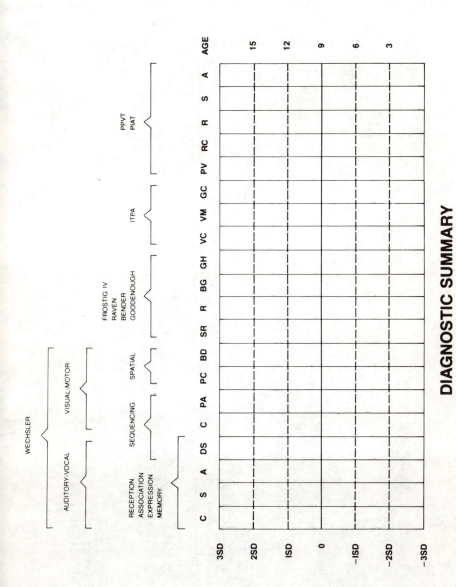

DIAGNOSTIC SUMMARY

Appendix:
Source Materials on Alternative Programs

Balfour, M. *School-based adolescent groups—The SAIL model.* EC 113 251.

Flood, H. *Accreditation report, Chana High School.*

Julia, V. *Bellefaire, a residential treatment center for children and adolescents.* EC 132 526.

Lear, R. *Alternative program handbook* (3rd Ed.). State College Area School District, State College PA. EC 132 524.

McCauley, R. *Longfellow Education Center referral manual.* EC 131 791.

Rissler, R. *Handbook of information and operational guidelines for William Smith High School.* EC 132 523.